About the Book

We all tell ourselves stories. These are stories about who we are, how the world works and how others relate to us. For better or worse, these stories often end up shaping our identities and framing our realities. That is why we should aspire to direct and channel these stories in a manner that is constructive and supportive of our goals and best interests. *Leading with Stories* presents a framework that enables the development and telling of positive and empowering stories that will help us respond effectively to the challenges and opportunities that life will through at us and equip us with social skills and mindsets that will empower us to be happy, prosperous and having a positive impact on the world. The book explores the role played by the language we use and the vocabulary and words we routinely utilise in creating and influencing the stories we tell ourselves and how these stories affect the way we carry ourselves and manage our relationships with others. Being aware of our internal narrative and cultivating the ability to take charge of it have always been a mark of success and effective leadership. This self-awareness and the ability to direct our internal narrative are also necessary for our wellbeing, resilience and flourishing.

As the nature of life and work continue to be shaped by technology, and as the value that we add to life continues to migrate from the physical and cognitive domains to the emotional domain, focusing on developing our individual and collective emotional potential is becoming a more pressing necessity. This has been accelerated by the latest advancements in Artificial Intelligence (A.I.), particularly the launch of ChatGPT in November 2022. As A.I. learns from us and becomes more capable of delivering many of the tasks humans used to perform, we are forced to question our cognitive superiority and even the future of our relevance. To remain relevant in a world defined by uncertainty and increasingly empowered by technology, we need to reach deep within ourselves to what makes us humans in order to guarantee that we continue to be capable of adding authentic and unique value to ourselves, our communities and life in general. For better or worse, technology has always been an extension of ourselves and our intentions. This is even more true in the case of A.I. To secure human success in the age of Artificial

Intelligence, we must bring to bear the best versions of ourselves and ensure that love, compassion, and wisdom prevail. This will necessitate intentionally building our positive leadership capacity. Defining leadership as the ability to inspire and influence through changing the internal narratives and stories told by individuals and teams, this book can be used by leaders, educators, parents and individuals to create positive change and inculcate emotional intelligence and attributes such as self-awareness, self-management, social awareness and relationship management within themselves and people under their care. These attributes are increasingly acknowledged as the bedrock of happiness, success and flourishing in life, whether in the competitive business world, school or home. This book is not about the development of Artificial Intelligence; however, it summarises the leadership qualities and outlines practical techniques needed to prosper in a world where Artificial Intelligence will be a crucial shaper for decades to come. The book provides easy-to-follow guides and well-structured exercises on how to develop empowering narratives and emotional intelligence at individual and organisational levels. It is based on the latest findings in neuroscience and refers to many success stories, both personal and organisational. The techniques described in the book were tried and successfully implemented by more than 5,000 students from over 150 countries who took my *Success with Emotional Intelligence* online course.

Leading with Stories is an updated edition of my previous book, which was published under the title *Shoot the Boss*. This edition further attempts to make the case for the importance of fostering human leadership skills, particularly developing a deep sense of personal purpose and storytelling, in an age where Artificial Intelligence disrupts life in all aspects. The book also features a new chapter dedicated to working with Artificial Intelligence.

Praise for "Leading with Stories"

"Delve into a masterful exploration of the art of storytelling for leaders with Mushtak's groundbreaking book. With eloquence and insight, he unveils the profound impact of storytelling– a skill transcending communication, becoming the very heart of transformative leadership. As our world evolves beyond the trials of the COVID-19 pandemic and humanity seeks meaning amidst the convergence of Artificial Intelligence and purposeful living, this book emerges as a guiding light.

Addressing CEOs, educators, parents and all poised for change, Mushtak's work beckons. Through lucid prose, practical exercises and inspiring stories, the book becomes an indispensable companion. Seamlessly navigating the realms of business adaptation and life's intricate tapestry, this book promises to empower and enrich."

Charles Brewer, Group Chief Executive Officer, Pos Malaysia

"Mushtak's approach to leadership, entrepreneurship and management has profoundly and positively impacted the lives of thousands of people worldwide. The first time I spoke to Mushtak, it was clear that he was a passionate educator who, for years, was inspiring and motivating the students where he lectured. However, it wasn't until he launched his first MOOC in 2013 that the rest of the world also got to know him. Through his MOOCs on entrepreneurship, emotional intelligence and thinking like an engineer, thousands of students rewired their brains to think positively, attempted to solve grand challenges with people they had never met and changed their lives by changing their vocabulary. Always looking for new and more effective ways to educate more students, Mushtak is an inspiration to educators and engineers worldwide. This curiosity led him to explore MOOCs and first brought me and Open Learning to Malaysia. So, while it's impossible to predict where you might go and what you might achieve, I'm sure Mushtak's approach will make an impact on you as well."

Adam Brimo, Founder and CEO, Open Learning

"An engineer by training and a change agent through experience, Mushtak brings his deep knowledge and frontline leadership experience to this engaging and thought-provoking examination of the role of happiness in everyday life. The book will appeal to everyone who seeks to explore their own purpose in life more deeply and to those who want to enjoy lasting success and personal fulfilment. The idea of the book is very simple: We all tell stories in our heads that end up shaping who we are. Great leaders and great companies are able to make people change their stories to be more positive and inspirational. As one of Mushtak's students most ably puts it, 'At the end of the day, the technical knowledge without a true-life understanding is the mechanics without any power.' If there is one takeaway from the book, it is the power each one of us has to shape our own future by simply changing the P[roblem] word to the O[pportunity] word. Enjoy your own journey to greater happiness in the company of Mushtak."

Graham Watson, Founder, Positive Leadership Limited

"This is a book everyone should read, regardless of who you are or what you do. Mushtak does a stellar job in summing up and converting the art of living a purposeful and successful life into science, easily replicated, scaled and shared. I love how this book combines new and old knowledge and concepts, making it relevant and, more importantly, easily applied. I believe any reader, just like me, would appreciate the attentive guidance provided throughout the process, from the introduction of concepts to the practical exercises in the book. I strongly recommend this as a handbook that all 21st century leaders carry along to better lead successful lives, families, teams and companies."

John-Son Oei, Founder and CEO, EPIC

"A book of fascinating insights. Mushtak puts the emphasis and lens on the critical importance of our storytelling and how we can use our minds to tell stories to increase our ability to shape and control our lives. This book is a great example. In itself, be it the style of the storytelling or the content, this book excels in engaging the mind in the pursuit of being personally more productive and positive in life. In helping us shape more formidable stories for ourselves and our teams.

I loved that this book inspired me to think differently and deeply. Elegantly blending emotional intelligence with neuroscience, it offers powerful and practical hints, tips, tools and techniques allied to both theories. While not all of them were new to me, I found myself continuously stopping to take notes on what I could use both myself and in my work with others; this is always a sign of a great book in my book! This book is at all times accessible to the reader even as it explores deep psychological human traits."

Mary Clarke, Director, Sticky Change

About the Author

Professor Mushtak Al-Atabi is currently the Provost and CEO at Heriot-Watt University Malaysia. A passionate educator, innovator and an agent of change, Mushtak always challenges the status quo to unlock value. He pioneered the use of the CDIO (Conceive, Design, Implement, Operate) educational framework in Malaysia. He offered one of the first Massive Open Online Courses (MOOCs) in Asia (the first in Malaysia) in 2013. His online classes, *Entrepreneurship, Success with Emotional Intelligence* and *Global Entrepreneurship*, attracted thousands of students from 150 countries. He speaks at international conferences and consults for national and multinational corporations, including universities, banks and manufacturing and energy companies, in the areas of leadership, innovation, human development, performance and technology. Mushtak is the author of *Think Like an Engineer* and *Driving Performance*. His research interests include thermo-fluids, renewable energy, biomechanical engineering, engineering education and academic leadership. He has numerous research publications, awards and honours. Mushtak is a Fellow of the Institution of Mechanical Engineers (UK), a member of the Board of Directors at the British Malaysia Chamber of Commerce and the Chairman of the Vice Chancellors' Council of Private Universities in Malaysia.

"I am a storyteller. My purpose is to inspire others to tell more empowering stories about themselves and the world we live in."

Impact Statement
Mushtak Al-Atabi

Leading with Stories

Securing Human Success in the Age of Artificial Intelligence

by

Mushtak Al-Atabi
Author of "Think Like an Engineer" and "Driving Performance"

DREAM BIG. BE DIFFERENT. HAVE FUN

ISBN: 978-967-13063-2-1

Published by:
Mushtak Al-Atabi
Heriot-Watt University Malaysia
No 1, Jalan Venna P5/2, Precinct 5
62200 Putrajaya, Malaysia

www.thinklikeanengineer.org

Acknowledgement

It is often said that it takes a village to raise a person. How true this sentiment is! Here, I would like to express my heartfelt appreciation to those who constitute my village. Without their contributions, this book and my other works would not have come to fruition. My deepest gratitude extends to all those who believed in me, guided me, provided their unwavering support, and influenced both my life journey and my way of thinking.

I wish to commence by acknowledging my family—my remarkable parents, my beloved wife, and my extraordinary sons, Sarmad, Furat, and Ayham. Additionally, I want to express my sincere thanks to my educators and the authors of the exceptional books that have shaped my reading journey.

I am also indebted to all my students, from whom I learned a great deal. Special recognition goes to those who have agreed to share their impactful and transformative stories featured in this book.

Contents

Foreword

Mushtak Al-Atabi is a pioneer in every sense, and he wants you to be one too. Part management theorist, part engineer, part self-appointed student of neuroscience, he points out, using numerous examples and proven theories, that if we want to change – to become happier, healthier, more effective, more self-aware – then we can.

It is hardly a surprise that someone whose Ph.D. thesis linked fluid mechanics to gallstones has such a grasp of how our biological functions affect our ability to lead and manage. I was first introduced to Mushtak's refreshing way of thinking when I watched his TEDx talk on how and why we should banish the word 'problem' from our vocabulary. (I have now banished it from mine – if you want to know why you should follow suit then look at YouTube). Watching him made me wish I had been one of the 5,000 students around the world who took his MOOC, *Success with Emotional Intelligence*. If, like me, you missed that particular boat, then no worries – read this book and you will encounter much of the learning (and even some of the students) from that course.

It might sound simplistic to suggest that rewiring our brain can be done simply by changing the language that we use, but Mushtak has gathered all the evidence to show exactly that. The stories in our head, he argues, end up shaping who we are. You can create those stories yourself; he does, often. The slightly alarming title of Chapter Ten, 'Shoot the Boss', refers to a paintball exercise he undertook to get his former university ready for its next round of accreditation. Staff were taken to the paintball venue and asked questions to indicate their readiness for the inspection. Every time they answered a question incorrectly, they had to shoot Mushtak, a punishment for him not having prepared them well enough. Flipped learning? No. Evidence that thinking differently produces results.

This book suggests that one sure sign of emotional intelligence is a genuine interest in developing others. That being so, Mushtak Al-Atabi must indeed have a very high EQ because this book is a complete roadmap to self-development. What story are you going to develop and tell? Read on and decide.

Professor Dame Heather McGregor,
Provost, Heriot-Watt University Dubai

Introduction

In 2013, I developed and offered a Massive Open Online Course (MOOC) entitled *Success with Emotional Intelligence*. The course aimed to introduce the concept of emotional intelligence to my engineering undergraduate students. Besides the engineering students in our school, the course was made available for free to anyone who wanted to enrol online. The course ended up having more than 5,000 students from over 150 different countries.

The *Success with Emotional Intelligence* course was designed and delivered to engineering students to address several needs. Firstly, as we educate engineers to Conceive, Design, Implement and Operate products, services, processes and systems that add value to and address the needs of users and customers, emotional intelligence is considered a necessary "skill" to enable students to work collaboratively as well as to foster empathy, which is a critical requirement in creating products and services that others will use. Secondly, employers have repeatedly indicated that emotional intelligence is something that they would like to see more of in graduates in general. Employers are increasingly realising that besides technical competencies, graduates need to possess emotional resilience, self-management, empathy and the ability to productively and effectively manage relationships. Furthermore, beyond the job market requirements, emotional intelligence is essential for individuals to lead happy and balanced lives. Against this background, and being an engineer, I started looking for a simple and robust methodology that can be used to introduce and teach emotional intelligence to engineering students. The emotional intelligence framework developed by Daniel Goleman met the requirements and fitted the bill nicely.

Goleman's framework for emotional intelligence has four domains: self-awareness, self-management, social awareness and relationship management. Each of these domains has a number of traits, and Daniel Goleman wrote a few bestselling books to explain and popularise the concept, including *Emotional Intelligence* and *Working with Emotional Intelligence*. When I started designing the course and developing its materials, I realised the need to translate the different traits of the emotional intelligence framework to structured learning activities that students can perform, experience and go through in order to grow their emotional intelligence. So, I played the role of a learning architect as I selected, developed and integrated various activities to be part of the students' learning journey.

The response of students from all over the world towards the course and its activities was phenomenal. Many have reported astonishing results related to improvements in their self-awareness, happiness and relationships with those around them. A survey to measure how the students perceived their emotional intelligence before and after the course indicated that the 18-week course generally resulted in improved levels of the different emotional intelligence traits. Even more interestingly, a decrease in emotional intelligence was reported when a similar survey was administered to a control group of university students who did not take the course. This drop in emotional intelligence is not entirely surprising as researchers have reported a decline in empathy, for example, in university students undertaking tertiary studies. This further underscores the need to include teaching emotional intelligence in the curriculum.

My involvement with emotional intelligence was supposed to be for a single course, but it ended up becoming a lifelong passion. I started reading, researching, writing and speaking about my experience with teaching emotional intelligence. And the more I explored it, the more it made sense. As the COVID-19 pandemic hit the world, I observed a surge in the need for and the recognition of the importance of teaching emotional intelligence to people of all ages and at all stages of life. Individuals, parents, educators and business leaders reached out to look for practical and accessible ways to improve competency levels in emotional intelligence.

In one way or another, we all value and pursue success and happiness; however, the harder we search for them, the more elusive they become. This can be a symptom of a significant breakdown in education systems worldwide that is characterised by the failure to prepare students to live happy and fulfilling lives. Very few schools and universities, if any, have academic programmes declaring, as part of their educational objectives, enabling their graduates to have balanced, fulfilling and happy lives. There can be a number of reasons for this observation, one of which is that academic institutions may not know what curriculum and pedagogy they should use to prepare graduates to lead happy and fulfilling lives. They may also assume that providing a good technical education, which will result in a good job and stable income, will eventually lead the students to achieve their potential and live the enriching lives they deserve.

I am not questioning the relevance of academic excellence and the importance of inculcating mastery of technical skills for doctors, engineers, accountants and other professionals. These skills are now expected as the basis of the educational provision. However, the latest developments in Artificial Intelligence and especially the release of ChatGPT in November of 2022, have demonstrated that in the future, these technical skills will be delivered, mainly in collaboration with machines, leaving humans with the need to dig deep to ensure that the value we are adding to life, relationships, and work is unique and special. The changing requirements of the time we live in, with its fast pace, complex connections and challenging nature, compel us to rethink and reconsider how we prepare ourselves and our youth for careers that leverage Artificial Intelligence and lives that transcend it. Investing in discovering, articulating and documenting our purpose and what brings meaning to our lives and building purpose-driven careers where we mobilise our purpose into a positive impact on the world will be the way to have sustained success, influence and happiness.

In his 2016 New Year message to educators, the Dalai Lama stressed the importance of educating children so that they may have a realistic opportunity to change the world.

"We all want happiness and to avoid suffering, and within ourselves that involves a greater sense of love and compassion. As far as the external world is concerned, it will entail taking serious steps to preserve the environment and adapt to climate change. These days, scientists are increasingly finding evidence that cultivating love and compassion positively affects our physical health and general well-being. Humanity is made up of individuals, and we will only achieve a happier, more peaceful society if those individuals are happier and more peaceful within themselves," the Dalai Lama said.

He goes on to add, "I am optimistic about this. I believe that human nature is fundamentally positive and again scientists are finding evidence to support this. Experiments with infants, who are too young to talk and so have limited conceptual thinking, show that they respond favourably to illustrations of people helping each other. They show clear adverse responses to illustrations of people harming or obstructing each other. What's more, scientists have shown that constant fear and anger have a damaging effect on our immune systems.

"We may conclude that human nature is essentially compassionate. Love and affection are essential because we all depend on others to survive. Therefore, affection is part of our basic nature. If it was otherwise and it was our nature to be angry and hateful, there would be little we could do, but because it is our nature to be affectionate and compassionate, it's possible for us to think of enhancing these natural qualities through education and training," the Dalai Lama concludes.

Another intriguing mystery worth exploring here is the seemingly weak correlation between Intelligence Quotient (IQ) and academic performance on one hand and real-life success on the other. This is symbolised by the observation that many of those with average IQs are able to outperform, in life and work, some of those with higher IQs. A solid body of research indicates that the missing link in this equation is emotional intelligence, which is usually possessed by highly successful individuals regardless of the level of their IQ. Emotional intelligence can be viewed as an amplifier of IQ. Therefore, individuals with a reasonable IQ but highly developed emotional intelligence will be better equipped to harness their potential and that of others, leading to higher added value and greater success.

There is a convergence of a number of undercurrents indicating that emotional intelligence is poised to be a central theme of this century. In a speech at Oxford University in May 2018, Andy Haldane, the then Chief Economist of the Bank of England, said: "Students may be better off developing emotional intelligence than cognitive skills to prepare for a future of work in which they will be competing against robots." Coming from the chief economist of one of the oldest central banks in the world, this is serious stuff. As a matter of fact, if the situation is framed as a competition between humans and machines, we may be heading in the direction of unfavourable outcomes. An alternative framing is to explore how we can help people acquire the skills and mindsets that will enable them to lead in an environment where humans can leverage machines and work with, rather than compete against, them. This way, both sides will be delivering what they are best at: machines excelling at their physical strength, precision, fast processing of vast amounts of data, and discerning of trends, and humans using their wisdom, judgement, intuition and applying their empathy, creativity, compassion, and the ability to build trust. I hope that more and more schools and academic institutions will start paying more attention to emotional intelligence and the development of the emotional wellbeing of their students when it comes to curriculum design and delivery.

Over the years, I received many requests from those who participated in the *Success with Emotional Intelligence* course and also those who listened to me speak about that course to compile the experiences that we had in a book. That is why I wrote *Shoot the Boss*. Since then, we have gone through a global pandemic and seen breathtaking advancements in A.I. This book is an enhanced edition of *Shoot the Boss* that presents an updated version of the work framed as a methodology for human development in the age of Artificial Intelligence.

This book has the purpose of introducing emotional intelligence in a practical manner. It offers exercises designed to cultivate and enhance emotional intelligence across diverse contexts, encompassing home, school, and workplace settings. The book also presents a holistic framework that explains how emotional intelligence is rooted in the narrative and language used by individuals and groups. This framework serves as a foundation for facilitating change management and fostering transformation, spanning individual as well as organisational dimensions.

The book starts by briefly describing our current understanding of how the brain works and the role of the language we use and our internal narrative in the way we think, feel, behave and manage our relationships. After introducing the framework that integrates language, narrative and emotional intelligence, stories illustrating how the framework can be used in various settings are provided. Many stories from the students who took the *Success with Emotional Intelligence* course are featured, too.

1

Homo Relator: What Makes Us Human

"It's like everyone tells a story about themselves inside their own head. Always. All the time. That story makes you what you are. We build ourselves out of that story."

Patrick Rothfuss, The Name of the Wind

As a child, the thickest book I owned was *The Arabian Nights*. It had a white hardcover and beautiful rough yellow papers and came in two volumes. I proudly displayed it on my bookshelf and read it over and over again. Even now, every time I think of that book, I can almost smell the distinctive scent of its pages. The book revolves around the story of King Shahryar, who lost trust in all women when he found out one day that his beloved wife was unfaithful to him. After executing her, he resolved to marry a new virgin each night and ordered her beheaded the next day. This way, the king would ensure that his wife would have no chance to be unfaithful. As the kingdom started to run out of virgins worthy of marrying the king, Scheherazade, the daughter of one of the state's top officials, offered herself to be the next bride and assured her father that she had a plan. Scheherazade was intelligent, beautiful, well-spoken and highly educated. She read books in many languages and knew stories from different and faraway kingdoms. On their first night as a married couple, Scheherazade offered to tell the king a story to entertain him, and the king accepted. The story was enchanting, entertaining, and captivating. Within the narrative, various characters shared their tales, allowing Scheherazade to ensure the continuation of the story. From the first night and continuing after that, Scheherazade skilfully halted the narrative just before dawn at carefully chosen cliffhanger moments, leaving the King eagerly anticipating more and yearning to discover what would unfold next. If Scheherazade were alive today, she would undoubtedly excel as a prominent writer for the Netflix series. Every time the king decides to postpone her death until she finishes her story, she remains alive for one more day. In her stories, animals spoke, magic lamps housed genies who fulfilled wishes, and flying carpets soared high. The story went on for one thousand and one nights, a time during which Scheherazade had children with the King and earned his trust, and ultimately, she saved her life and the lives of many other innocent girls.

While the stories in *The Arabian Nights* are but a collection of myths, it is not only King Shahryar who is captivated by a good story; good stories fascinate all of us. That is why we watch movies and find listening to gossip irresistible. Our love for stories seems to have a neurological basis, and I shall devote this chapter to exploring the human brain from a storytelling angle. This will be helpful as we attempt to develop the framework that will enable us to understand how narratives and stories shape who we are and how they are grounded in the way our brains are wired. I will also dedicate space to explore how we can influence the stories told at individual and organisational levels so that they are anchored in our higher purpose to enable the achievement of success, happiness and a positive impact on the world.

The Human Brain

The human brain is the most complex and remarkable object in the known universe. While it weighs around 2% of the body weight, it consumes 20% of the energy used by the body. On average, it has 85 billion neurons, and those neurons have the ability to connect with each other in endless ways and configurations. These limitless connection patterns and interactive possibilities among the neurons enable the electrochemical activities that give rise to all our mental capacities, emotions, thoughts, memories, consciousness and the emergence of the mind itself.

We have always considered the human brain to be an essential component in making us who we are and recognised that it differentiates us from other animals. The brain is behind both intelligence and consciousness, the combination of which makes us the special species we are. Efforts to understand how the brain works and how we think were dedicated by philosophers, neurologists, psychologists, cognitive scientists and even engineers and computer scientists. The National Academy of Engineering (NAE) in the United States declared "Reverse engineering the human brain" as one of the Grand Challenges for Engineers in the 21st century [1]. The last few decades represented a golden era for our understanding of how the brain works. While we are still far from unlocking many of the brain's mysteries, we managed to have unprecedented access to how the human brain works and how it is structured and organised. Scientists from various domains are continuing their diligent efforts in the pursuit of the ultimate explanation of what makes us humans.

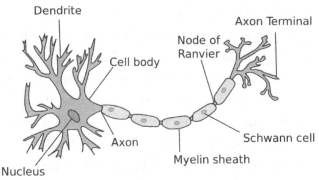

The neuron (Source: Wiki Commons)

Brain Functions and Structure

Neurological research has made many advances in recent decades, backed by technological wonders such as fMRI (Functional Magnetic Resonance Imaging) machines, where an individual's brain is scanned while that individual is performing a particular mental task. Knowing which part of the brain is engaged when each cognitive task is completed, we can map different areas of the brain to the variety of activities we perform and approximately know which part of the brain is activated when we are engaged in a particular mental activity. Studying brain disorders and traumas also contributed to our understanding of how the brain works. Patients who have sustained damage to specific parts of their brains due to trauma or stroke may experience a loss of certain brain functions. This allows us to infer that the particular area of the brain that has been damaged plays a role in the function that has been lost or affected.

The prevailing understanding of the human brain is that it represents a plastic and very flexible system. It has tremendous growth and learning potential. It continues to change throughout an individual's lifetime, responding to different challenges and performance requirements and continuously forming new connections between its neurons. Neurons are responsible for transferring electrochemical signals within the nervous system, enabling the emergence of the mind and the computing power of the brain that manifests itself as thoughts, predictions, decisions, memories, emotions and physical activities. The brain's flexibility is an attribute of its capability to create billions upon billions of combinations of connections between brain neurons as we learn new things and have repeated experiences. It is now well established that we can "sculpt" our brains to be happy, positive and successful through intentional actions, practice, and mental and emotional exercises that will result in the establishment of certain favourable neural connections that support positive habits and attitudes.

One way to imagine the neurons in the brain is to imagine a bundle of electrical wires. Some of these wires are well insulated, but a considerable number of them lack proper insulation. Consequently, as signals pass through, some neurons tend to leak electrical charges to adjacent neurons, weakening the signal as it passes through. That is why when we start learning a new skill, for example, riding a bicycle, it feels awkward at the beginning as the signals carried from the brain to different parts of the body get weakened along the way, but as we keep on repeating and practising, a substance called myelin starts to form around the pathway of the electrical signal as it travels. Myelin is an electrical insulator, and as more layers of myelin are wrapped around the neuronal pathway, an equivalent of a signal highway is created, where very high-speed neuron firing can occur. This is the reason why we get better at doing things as we practice them, and this is also why it is difficult to change habits. In neuroscience, the saying goes, "Neurons that fire together, wire together."

Myelin formation starts in the 14th week of embryonic development and continues throughout life. The growth of myelin during the embryonic stage ensures the "programming" of the basic capabilities that an infant will need upon birth. Compared to babies of other animals, human babies are born more vulnerable and with little capabilities; a baby gazelle, for example, is born able to stand, walk and even run shortly after birth, while a human baby needs months before they begin taking their first steps. This is an indication that the neuro-circuitry for walking is yet to be myelinated in humans upon birth. Although this may seem like a disadvantage at first, in fact, the lack of myelination at birth is a powerful advantage. It gives the human brain unlimited potential as we can programme our brains by inducing the formation of myelin through neuron firing. This makes the human brain highly adaptable and enables individuals to master highly diversified skills and professions.

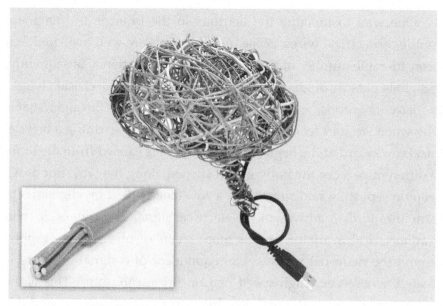

Myelin is like the insulation around electric wires

So, whether learning how to paint, how to play the piano, or how to drive a car, we are essentially building myelin around the pathways of the electrical signals needed to control the muscles responsible for performing these tasks. Myelination results in better, faster and more targeted neuron firing sequences, hence mastery of the skill. Interestingly, the same process works for intentional and non-intentional actions, so if we keep on repeating a routine long enough, myelination will lead to the wiring of our habits and mental models, whether we are aware of this or not.

As mentioned earlier, the brain is highly complex, and our journey to understand its structure and organisation, let alone its functions, is still at its beginning. However, for the purpose of this book, a simplistic categorisation of the brain structure is both useful and sufficient. There are generally two ways to categorise the brain structure: bottom-up and left-right. These are outlined in the sections below.

The Brain from the Bottom Up

If we take a cross-section of the brain along the body's plane of symmetry, three distinctive brain regions can be identified. The first brain region is the brain stem, which is the bridge between the spinal cord and the brain and the gateway for all signals and sensations coming into and out of the brain. Because it is similar to the brains of reptiles, this brain region is called the reptilian or old brain. Sitting on top of the old brain is the next brain region called the middle brain, followed by the final brain layer, the new brain. If you imagine the brain as a cone of ice cream, the first scoop will represent the old brain, the second scoop will represent the middle brain, and the new brain will be represented by the third scoop. It is useful here to mention that mental activities are the result of very complex processes and interactions, and often, even the most straightforward decision involves multiple areas of the brain working together. Now, let us examine the main features of each brain region from the bottom up.

The Old Brain

The old brain is directly connected to the spinal cord. In this part of the brain, the basic survival instincts are hardwired. The old brain operates in a rather automatic manner and gets activated in the event of perceived danger and life-threatening conditions. We have very little conscious control over this area of the brain. The old brain is responsible for the split-second decisions we make when a car is about to hit us or if we suspect that a venomous snake is about to attack us. The old brain is focused on survival; it gets triggered when we feel danger and instantly responds to negative stimuli. If we were to describe it briefly, we could say it is fast and selfish because it acts quickly and only in self-interest. As it represents the gateway to the other parts of the brain, the old brain takes over our reactions in case of danger and responds automatically. This is what we call the fight or flight response.

The Middle Brain

The middle brain is the part of the brain where emotions reside and are managed and where social cues are processed. It is responsible for processing how we feel and is incapable of analysing language (more about language processing in the next section). This may be the reason why we often find it difficult to express our feelings and emotions in words. This part of the brain plays a crucial role in decision-making. Contrary to the common belief, humans make many of the moment-to-moment decisions based on emotional rather than rational reasons. From a computational point of view, this simplifies and quickens the decision-making process. This has enormous implications for politicians, marketers and educators who would like to influence the behaviour of others. We vote, buy and learn when we "like" what we see, hear and what we are presented with.

The New Brain

The outermost layer of the brain, the new brain, is the part of the brain that is mainly responsible for high-level reasoning, such as mathematics, language, perception, imagination, art, music, and planning. It is very analytical and slows the process of decision-making. It is the rational brain, also called the neocortex. This layer of the brain is fully developed only in humans, and it's what sets us well apart from other primates.

Emotions

Stimuli that our environments throw at us are transferred as electrical signals that travel through the nervous system and the spinal cord to the brain. Everything we touch, smell, hear and see follows this pathway. The old brain is the first part of the brain that receives incoming signals. This enables us to subconsciously and quickly assess and respond to what we perceive as threatening situations as the old brain takes over our responses. Stimuli that are not perceived as threatening progress further into the brain to the next stage, the middle brain. You can imagine that such architecture was very beneficial for our ancient ancestors who lived in danger-filled environments and needed to make fight-or-flight decisions on a daily basis.

Signals that don't seem to be conveying danger will progress through the middle brain to be processed for emotions and social cues contained in them. Only after passing through the middle brain will signals reach the new brain for further processing.

Let's try to convey this with an example. Suppose you were walking towards your next appointment in the city and heard someone shouting behind you while rushing to reach you. Your first reaction, processed through your old brain, might be fear and anxiety. Your heartbeat accelerates, and you may turn around to investigate what is going on. As the middle brain kicks in, you are trying to assess if the person is shouting in anger or excitement, using other social and emotional cues you may gather as the situation develops. If the situation is still unclear, the new brain gets engaged. Could this be the cashier from the coffee shop where you just bought your ice blended coffee, and they are giving you back your phone, which you have just realised you forgot at the coffee shop? Suddenly, you feel happy and grateful and start thanking the person profusely.

This architecture of the brain has profound implications for the role of emotions in thinking and how we can rewire our brains. As signals go through the old and middle brains before reaching the new brain, emotions will always colour our thoughts and impact our decisions. As the new brain is the only part of the brain that is capable of processing language, we can force the flow of signals to be directed to it by describing our emotions using language. So, while our old brain always asks questions of the order: Is this dangerous? Is this bad for me? We can always use our language to train our brains to build more positive thought patterns that reduce our stress levels and help us realise the abundant opportunities available all around us.

As mentioned earlier, contrary to common belief, the emotional brain plays a key role in the decisions that we make. This was illustrated by the case of a patient known in neuroscience literature as Elliot. Elliot had surgery to remove a small tumour from his brain. His doctors were very pleased to note that the surgery did not adversely impact Elliot's cognitive capacities or speech. However, strange things started happening to Elliot after the operation. He began to debate every detail of his life endlessly. Decisions such as which shirt to wear or which way to take to work took Elliot hours to ponder. Even simple things like using a black or blue pen to write became stressful decisions, and Elliot weighed all their pros and cons before settling on the colour to use. Elliot was eventually sacked from his job, and his wife divorced him. A closer examination by neuroscientists revealed that although Elliot's new brain was doing an excellent job at the rational side of decision-making, the surgery somehow disconnected Elliot from his emotional brain. Losing that "gut feeling" or "like or dislike" feeling that we all have when faced with everyday life decisions rendered Elliot incapable of making any decision without going through a detailed analysis. Elliot's story shows that to lead happy and successful lives, all parts of our brains must work together in harmony. It is also essential to understand the limitations of our thinking so that we can improve its quality.

The above quick and brief description will be helpful as we explore topics such as emotional intelligence, communication, teamwork and human interaction later in this book. A basic understanding of the thinking process and the brain functions and structure are essential for all of us, particularly as A.I. continues to develop and disrupt life, making the need to know how to leverage A.I. capabilities and appreciate what makes us unique more pressing. It is helpful to reiterate here that the brain works like an orchestra, with all its parts contributing to the thinking symphony. So, the three brain regions are constantly collaborating to respond to the continuous stream of stimuli we call life.

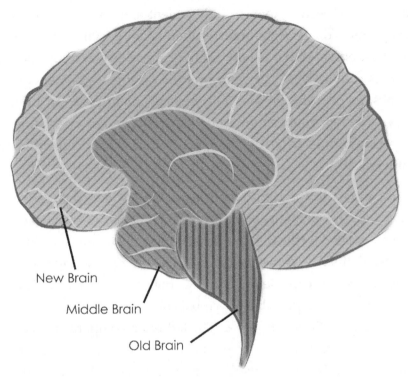

New Brain

Middle Brain

Old Brain

The Old, Middle and New Brain

Left Brain, Right Brain, Split Brain

Besides the three layers of brain tissue that we discussed in the previous section, we know that the brain has two different hemispheres: the left (which controls the right half of the body) and the right (which controls the left half of the body). These two hemispheres are connected by a tissue bridge called the corpus callosum. While we feel like a single individual with a single brain, in many ways, we have two brains. Thoughts, memories, and emotions cascade throughout the entire brain, but some tasks are handled better by one side of the brain than the other.

The right hemisphere is mainly in charge of spatial abilities and image processing, which includes recognising faces. It also processes music and interprets context and tone of voice. The right hemisphere thinks in images, focuses on the big picture, and, most interestingly, is

17

incapable of speech. It lives in the moment and has little concept of passing time. For the right brain, each moment is rich with emotions and sensations, and that is how we have the ability to remember key moments of our lives. The right brain is carefree, spontaneous and very absorbed in the present and what possibilities it can bring. It relishes finding connections and relationships amongst different concepts, which is why it is often associated with imagination and creativity.

In contrast to the right hemisphere, the left hemisphere is very methodical and analytical. It thrives on details. It takes the rich moments created by the right brain and strings them into a meaningful sequence that tells a coherent story. Unlike the right hemisphere, the left hemisphere is capable of handling spoken language, and it is the part of our brain responsible for verbal communication and the inner dialogue we continuously have. The left brain compares the current moment to the past and tries to predict the future, creating the concept of time. It spends most of its time analysing the past and pondering the future, and it excels at logic and mathematics and retrieving factual information from memory.

It is worth mentioning here that functional differentiation between the two brain hemispheres largely holds in the majority of the population. Still, there exists a small minority of individuals who have their brain hemispheric functions reversed.

The Harvard brain scientist Jill Taylor reported her experiences of having a stroke in her book *My Stroke of Insight*. On the morning of the stroke, she had a haemorrhage in her left brain that periodically took her left brain offline, allowing her to experience her being as perceived by her right brain alone. She described this in a TED talk she gave after her full recovery. "… I lost my balance, and I'm propped up against the wall. I look down at my arm, and I realise that I can no longer define the boundaries of my body. I can't define where I begin and where I end because the atoms and the molecules of my arm blended with the atoms and molecules of the wall. And all I could detect was this energy." Jill told a fascinated audience.

"And I'm asking myself, 'What is wrong with me? What is going on?' And in that moment, my left hemisphere brain chatter went totally silent, just like someone took a remote control and pushed the mute button—total silence. And at first, I was shocked to find myself inside of a silent mind. But then, I was immediately captivated by the magnificence of the energy around me. And because I could no longer identify the boundaries of my body, I felt enormous and expansive. I felt at one with all the energy that was, and it was beautiful there.

"Then all of a sudden, my left hemisphere comes back online, and it says to me, 'Hey! We've got a problem! We've got to get some help.' And I'm going, 'Ahh! I've got a problem!' So, it's like, 'OK, I've got a problem.' But then I immediately drifted right back out into the consciousness, and I affectionately refer to this space as 'La La Land'. But it was beautiful there. Imagine what it would be like to be totally disconnected from your brain chatter that connects you to the external world." Jill said. [2]

It is helpful to reiterate here that while different hemispheres are better equipped to handle specific mental tasks, it's the collaboration and the back-and-forth bouncing of electric signals that result in the emergence of our minds and our personalities. Strange things happen when a person's brain hemispheres are disconnected, making the information transfer between the two hemispheres impossible. The procedure to surgically sever the two hemispheres of the brain is called corpus callosotomy and is sometimes performed as a last resort to treat severe epilepsy, which is untreatable using drugs. This procedure was pioneered by Dr. William P. van Wagenen in the 1940s. It was based on the insight provided by the observation that some patients with severe epileptic seizures show improvement when a tumour grows in their corpus callosum, an indication that dampening the storm of electrical exchange between the two brain hemispheres reduces the overall electrical activity and improves the epileptic condition.

Patients with split brains appear normal with no observable behavioural or cognitive change. They are able to keep their jobs and engage in meaningful interactions and conversations with others. These patients also provide an exciting promise of furthering our understanding of the human brain and its workings. Psychologist Michael Gazzaniga at the University of California at Santa Monica was one of the first researchers, alongside Roger Sperry, to enlist the help of split-brain patients in his work. In his book *Tales from Both Sides of the Brain*, Michael Gazzaniga describes many experiments he pioneered to understand split-brain patients. [3]

In one experiment, patients were put in front of a screen designed to flash certain words to either the left or the right visual fields. When the word "face" is flashed to the left eye and the patients asked what they saw, they answered that they did not know. Strangely enough, if they were asked to draw what they saw using their left hands, they would doddle a face. Then, seeing the doodled face with both eyes, they would realise they saw a face. What happened here is that the word "face" was processed by the right hemisphere of the brain, which is incapable of speech. The same hemisphere, however, controls the left hand, and that is how it was able to draw what the right hemisphere saw.

In other words, the two brain hemispheres' interaction that was supposed to happen through the corpus callosum took place on the paper where the face was doodled. It is now well documented that the sense of normalcy exhibited by split-brain patients results from the two brains queuing each other. So, when a signal to stand up is initiated by the left brain, the right half of the body starts the sequence for standing up. Sensing the impending motion, the right brain instructs the muscles in the left half of the body to respond appropriately and so on. Therefore, the communication between the two hemispheres occurs outside the brain without the brain realising that.

These experiments performed by Gazzaniga led him to a lifetime passion for studying the split-brain condition. He kept on designing more experiments through which he literally spoke to each hemisphere of the brain individually without the knowledge of the other hemisphere!

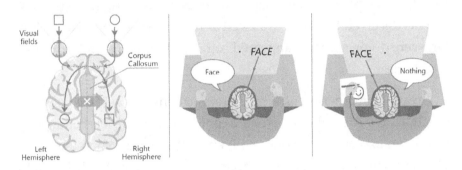

Split-brain experiment

In another experiment, split-brain patients were shown the words "bell" to the left visual field (right brain) and "music" to the right visual field (left brain). When the patients were asked to select an image related to what they saw from a list of four photos using their left hand, they pointed to the image with a bell. They ignored other photos with even closer musical connections, such as a piano, a violin, and a trumpet. This is expected as the right brain, which received the visual from the left eye, instructed the left hand to point at the photo with a bell as it is unaware that the word "music" was flashed to the left brain.

The amazing thing is that when the patients were asked why they chose the image of the bell, the left brain (the one capable of speech) confabulated a story that made sense of their choice by saying something like "It was because the last music I heard was coming from the college's bell towers." The right brain saw a bell (through the left eye) and told the left hand to point to it, but the left brain saw the word music and was now fabricating an explanation for disregarding the other pictures that were better related to the music theme.

The side of the brain in charge of speaking (left brain) saw the other side point out the bell, but instead of saying it didn't know why, it made up a reason! The right side was no wiser, so it went along with the fabrication. The patients were not telling lies or trying to be deceptive. They genuinely believed what they were saying. These patients deceived themselves as well as the researcher but had no idea they were doing so. They appeared congruent and never felt confused or dishonest.

In another experiment, a split-brain patient was asked to perform an action only the right hemisphere could see, and the left hemisphere once again explained it away as if it knew the cause. When the words "stand up" were displayed to the left eye, the patient stood. Asked by the researcher why he got up, the subject said, "I need to get a drink." When the same patient's right brain was asked to wave, he did that, and when asked why he waved, he said, "I thought I saw a friend." In another test, a violent scene depicting someone being pushed into the fire was displayed to only the right hemisphere (through the left eye). When asked to describe her emotions, the subject said she felt nervous, fearful and uneasy and attributed her feelings to how the room was decorated.

We now know that the left side of the brain, where speech is processed for the majority of people, is also responsible for interpreting our experiences and behaviours as well as making sense of what we are doing and going through. It is responsible for narrating and directing the story of our lives and our existence, ensuring that we remain sane. It helps us make sense of the world and our role in it, how we interact with other people, and our surrounding circumstances.

As discussed in the previous section, emotions are processed deeper in the brain (in the middle brain, closer to where the brain connects with the spinal cord). This implies that the brain tissue from both hemispheres could still communicate at a deeper level, even when the corpus callosum is severed. However, only the left hemisphere is able to describe the undercurrent of our existence and explain what both hemispheres are instructing the body to do.

Neurotransmitters

In our exploration of the functions and landscape of the brain, it is important to mention neurotransmitters which play a crucial role in communication between neurons. Neurotransmitters facilitate signal transmission across synapses, where tiny gaps between neurons exist. A balanced presence of these chemical messengers is necessary for our mental and physical health as they impact our moods, emotions, motivation, motor control as well as pain and sleep regulation. Through all of this, they clearly wield a profound influence on our health, relationships and our overall success. Let us embark on a brief journey through the roles and significance of the main neurotransmitters:

1. Serotonin: Often referred to as the "feel-good" neurotransmitter, serotonin plays a central role in regulating mood and emotions. It contributes to feelings of happiness, well-being, and contentment. Balanced serotonin levels are associated with a positive outlook on life and healthy relationships. Low serotonin levels can lead to mood disorders like depression and anxiety.

2. Dopamine: Dopamine is linked to the brain's reward and pleasure centres. It plays a key role in motivation, goal-setting, and the experience of pleasure. In relationships, dopamine can lead to feelings of infatuation and attachment. A well-functioning dopamine system can boost productivity and drive, contributing to success in various aspects of life.

3. Oxytocin: Often called the "love hormone" or "bonding hormone," oxytocin is released during social interactions and physical touch, such as hugging or cuddling. It fosters emotional connections, trust, and intimacy in relationships. Oxytocin is also associated with maternal-infant bonding and plays a role in childbirth and breastfeeding.

4. Noradrenaline: Noradrenaline is involved in the body's stress response and the "fight or flight" reaction. It can heighten alertness, focus and arousal. In relationships, it can lead to increased passion and excitement but can also contribute to stress and anxiety when overactive.

5. GABA (Gamma-Aminobutyric Acid): GABA is an inhibitory neurotransmitter that helps calm the brain and reduce anxiety. It counterbalances the effects of excitatory neurotransmitters. Adequate GABA levels are essential for emotional stability, relaxation, and stress management.

6. Endorphin: Endorphin is released during exercise, pain, stress, and pleasure. It acts as a natural painkiller and mood enhancer. Engaging in physical activity or experiencing enjoyable activities can boost endorphin levels, leading to improved emotional wellbeing and overall success.

7. Glutamate: Glutamate is the primary excitatory neurotransmitter in the brain, playing a role in learning, memory, and cognitive function. Balancing glutamate levels is crucial for mental clarity and emotional stability.

In summary, these neurotransmitters work together to shape our emotional experiences, enhance our relationships, and contribute to our success in various aspects of life. An imbalance in these neurotransmitters can lead to emotional and mental health issues, affecting our overall wellbeing and the quality of our relationships and achievements. Therefore, maintaining a healthy balance of neurotransmitters through lifestyle choices, including exercise, nutrition, and stress management, is essential for emotional resilience and success.

Homo Sapiens or Homo Relator?

The scientific name we modestly gave to our species is Homo Sapiens, which means "Wise Man" in Latin. This is based on the assumption that we are rational beings when it comes to how we lead our lives, make our decisions and choose between alternatives. Interestingly, recent scientific work started challenging this assumption, and while we are very intelligent creatures, we might be far from being the rational beings we claim to be. Instead, it is our ability to collaborate with others that makes us stand out and enables our intelligence to flourish. This collaboration is often powered by the common stories that we tell. Hence, a better name for our species might be Homo Relator or Storytelling Man. We shall explore this concept further in the following pages.

You may have noticed that you always talk to yourself in your mind. This relentless inner dialogue starts from the moment you wake up until you fall asleep. Almost everybody does this, and it is very normal. As explained earlier, this is your left brain doing its job of making sense of your existence. It is working on creating a coherent story of your life, just as it was elucidated by the split-brain patients. This inner dialogue represents the undercurrent of our thinking, how we see the world, and how we apply our logic and values to situations, people and events. Simply put, this inner or internal dialogue is the series of stories that we tell ourselves. These stories can fall into two main categories: the first contains stories about who we are and what we are capable of, and the second is about how the world around us works and interacts with us. These two stories are significant as they make up our identity and how we perceive and work with others and operate in the world. Our values are woven into these stories, and we craft them over a lifetime. Events and experiences, as well as other

25

people, contribute to the storyline. In her book *My Stroke of Insight*, Jill Taylor, whose TED talk we explored earlier, described how the stroke affected her left hemisphere, took her left brain offline and stopped her internal dialogue. "In this altered state of being, my mind was no longer preoccupied with the billions of details that my brain routinely used to define and conduct my life in the external world. Those little voices, that brain chatter that customarily kept me abreast of myself in relation to the world outside of me, were delightfully silent. And in their absence, my memories of the past and my dreams of the future evaporated. I was alone. In the moment, I was alone with nothing but the rhythmic pulse of my beating heart." [4]

In summary, the left brain interprets our experiences and tells stories that represent an essential mechanism for creating our identities and even our realities. This interpreter system weaves the meaning and values we believe in into stories that ultimately drive how we manage our responses to what life throws at us, how we perceive ourselves, what we are capable (or incapable) of and how we develop our relationships with others.

These stories are told both at individual levels as well as the group levels. As a matter of fact, narratives and stories told at the community level are essential for it to function effectively. In large groups, such as nations and societies where not everyone is directly related, or at least personally knows everyone else, holding on to common narratives and stories is indispensable.

This realisation can have a profound impact on how we perceive human performance, success, achievement and happiness, both at individual and group levels. It can help parents, educators and leaders motivate those under their care and transform individuals, organisations and communities by enabling them to achieve their full potential.

The ability to understand how our brains work and how to direct our internal narratives to motivate and empower ourselves and others is becoming even more critical at a time when the latest Artificial Intelligence developments are promising to transform our world and how we function within it. In a book published by the Club of Rome in 1979 titled *No Limits to Learning: Bridging the Human Gap*, James Botkin and his collaborators wrote: "The human gap is the distance between growing complexity and our capacity to cope with it. Clearly, one eternal human endeavour has been to develop additions to knowledge and improvements in action to deal with a complexity that, for most of history, derived primarily from natural phenomena. An essential difference today is that contemporary complexity is caused predominantly by human activities. We call it a human gap because it is a dichotomy between a growing complexity of our own making and a lagging development of our own capacities." [5]

This still rings true as we live through a unique historical moment. The technological advancements that our civilisation has achieved are exposing and widening our human gap, and we need to reach out to humanity's ultimate domain, our emotional potential, to save the day. In order for us to bridge the gap, remain relevant and also build technology without the risk of damaging our environment and threatening our very existence, we need to refocus our priorities, starting with our education system and leadership development.

In the following chapters, we will develop a framework that is aimed at understanding how stories and language drive human behaviour, performance and achievement. The framework is intended to enable us to flourish through balancing success and achievements with happiness, purpose, meaning and positive relationships.

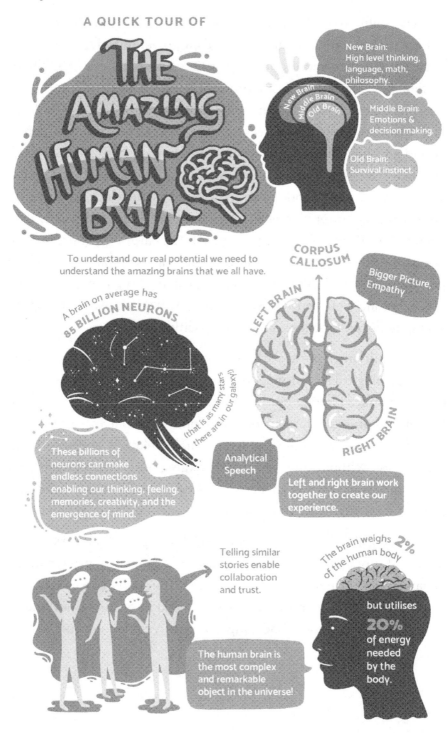

A QUICK TOUR OF

THE AMAZING HUMAN BRAIN

New Brain: High level thinking, language, math, philosophy.

New Brain
Middle Brain
Old Brain

Middle Brain: Emotions & decision making.

Old Brain: Survival instinct.

To understand our real potential we need to understand the amazing brains that we all have.

A brain on average has
85 BILLION NEURONS

(that is as many stars there are in our galaxy!)

These billions of neurons can make endless connections enabling our thinking, feeling, memories, creativity, and the emergence of mind.

CORPUS CALLOSUM

LEFT BRAIN

RIGHT BRAIN

Bigger Picture, Empathy

Analytical Speech

Left and right brain work together to create our experience.

Telling similar stories enable collaboration and trust.

The brain weighs **2%** of the human body

but utilises **20%** of energy needed by the body.

The human brain is the most complex and remarkable object in the universe!

2

How to Flourish in the Age of A.I.

"And I must say, there was both freedom and challenge for me in recognising that our perception of the external world, and our relationship to it, is a product of our neurological circuitry. For all those years of my life, I really had been a figment of my own imagination!"

Jill Taylor, My Stroke of Insight

For the first half of the twentieth century, the prevailing belief within the athletic community was that it was impossible to run the mile in under 4 minutes. Not difficult, not dangerous, but outright impossible! The athletic community thought that the human body couldn't physically go that fast and that it would collapse under pressure if such an attempt were made. This was the conventional wisdom, the story that doctors, scientists and athletes told, and the whole world accepted, that is, until Roger Bannister broke the record on 5 May 1956, achieving a time of 3:59.4 seconds. On that day, Bannister did not simply break the record. He literally changed the story. Suddenly, the 4 minutes was no longer a barrier, and the new story became "with hard work, planning and relentless execution and training, the 4-minute record can be broken." This had an immediate, profound impact on the track and field athletes; just 46 days after Bannister broke the record, Australian John Landy beat his time. The time to run the mile kept reducing, and currently, Hicham El Guerrouj is the men's record holder with a time of 3:43.13 seconds.

Almost immediately after Roger Bannister breached the 4-minute barrier, other athletes did the same. This is a testament to how powerful mental barriers can be when it comes to what we can do and how changing the stories we tell ourselves can change our reality. Clearly, the most important impact of Roger Bannister's achievement is the mental change it created in the minds of the athletes and the athletic community at large. This ability to tell and believe stories seems to be a uniquely human attribute that is a function of the human mind.

We shall return to this theme of the stories we tell within our minds repeatedly in this book as we develop the framework that describes how the language we use and the stories we tell impact our performance in life. These stories affect how we manage ourselves and our relationships, for better or worse and how we can be in control of the entire dynamic.

The human outlook consists of two primary constructs, namely self-management, the way we behave and deal with ourselves, as well as relationship management or how we treat others and how effectively we work and interact with them. These two constructs are highly affected by our internal narratives and the stories we humans tell. If you imagine our existence as an iceberg, self-management and relationship management can represent the visible part, while the stories that are told in the background of the mind are in the submerged part. It is easier to explain how this structure works with a negative example. In times of war and conflict where horrific crimes such as genocide are perpetrated, researchers observed that these crimes are always preceded by a change in how the perpetrators perceive the victims. In order for humans to inflict harm on other human beings, something that is against our nature, stories need to be told first, positioning those at the receiving end of the oppression as less than humans. In his book *Less than Human*, David Livingstone Smith explains that "human beings have long conceived of the universe as a hierarchy of value, with God at the top and inert matter at the bottom, and everything else in between." That model of the universe "doesn't make scientific sense," says Smith, but "nonetheless, for some reason, we continue to conceive of the universe in that fashion, and we relegate non-human creatures to a lower position on the scale." [1]

Then, within the human category, stories about hierarchy have been told, enabling atrocities such as slavery, the holocaust and multiple genocides. These stories evolve gradually with catastrophic consequences. They often start by saying "we" are different from "them" and move on to stereotyping the "others" by calling them names and describing them as animals and less than human. The pattern is well documented, and it has repeated itself again and again. While this book is not about the phenomena of dehumanisation, one can't but admit the power of stories we tell ourselves about "us", the "others", and the world we occupy in making ordinary people do extraordinary things, both for better and worse.

Interestingly, we can and should play an active role in writing and directing our stories, as some stories are more positive and helpful than others. Happy, successful and achieved people tell themselves positive stories about the world and their role in it. Their stories go along the lines of "I am full of capabilities, and I can learn how to deal with different situations in life. People are essentially good, and I can work with them to achieve our common goals. The world is full of resources, and I can use those to add value and achieve success for myself and others." Compare this to a story like "I am not lucky, and learning is always difficult for me. The world is full of people who want to take advantage of me." These stories could help individuals achieve their potential or limit it altogether. They are behind our most significant successes as well as our major failures and conflicts.

Influential leaders not only tell themselves compelling stories about the world, but more importantly, they can rally those with them around these stories. They have the ability to change the stories of the rest of us, and through this, they initiate the creation of a better future. The stories these influential leaders tell paint an uplifting future we can all be part of. These stories even depict a world where opportunities are abundant, and learning takes place alongside risk-taking and failures. These stories and the positive mental habits they generate and cultivate impact how a leader speaks, behaves and models the way, resulting in an embodied image of the desired state.

The world faces multiple existential challenges, including the climate emergency, growing inequality, and numerous stresses caused by health, economic and geopolitical crises. These interrelated challenges are making the world more complex and uncertain than ever. But even among that complexity and uncertainty, those of us with a positive outlook believe that we need to aim at shaping and creating a world that is sustainable, equitable, and enjoyable. Our stories will be a key part of realising that.

A Framework for Human Development and Performance

Many fundamental components for attaining effectiveness, success, and happiness in life aren't groundbreaking revelations; they've been well-known and deliberated upon for generations. Ideas such as establishing clear goals, practising discipline, nurturing positive relationships, demonstrating kindness to others, and prioritising self-care are not novel inventions. However, the paradox lies in the fact that despite the accessibility of this wisdom, a significant majority of individuals struggle to integrate these principles into their lives consistently.

This gap between knowledge and action is where the domain of human development and personal growth assumes a central role. Experts in this field, encompassing psychologists, life coaches and educators, endeavour to bridge this divide by offering guidance, tools, and support to aid individuals in surmounting obstacles, reshaping habits and cultivating the mindsets and behaviours essential for a flourishing life. In essence, the work on human development exists within the transformative space situated between timeless wisdom and the challenge of practical implementation, facilitating individuals in unlocking their full potential and leading more purposeful lives.

I hope we have established that the stories told within our left brain drive our behaviour to a large extent. Tell positive, empowering stories, and this will be reflected in the way you engage with the world. The building blocks of our stories are the words we use. After all, language is what the left brain uses for its internal chatter. Noam Chomsky, the American linguist, philosopher and cognitive scientist, believes that language evolved primarily as a mode of creating, processing and interpreting thought. While language is used for communication, it is basically a system of thought, and communication does not seem to be part of its design. According to Chomsky, "If you look carefully at the structure of language, you will find case after case, right at the core of language design, where there is a conflict between what would be efficient for communication and what is efficient for the specific biological design of the language and in every case, that is known, communicative efficiency is sacrificed. It is just not a consideration. This conclusion has a widespread significance."

One of the key themes of this book is the proposed framework for human development, performance and growth, shown in the figure below. It resembles an iceberg, with the lower levels influencing, driving and supporting the levels above. The different levels are described in the following sections.

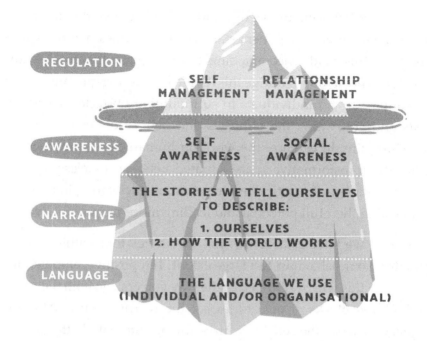

Framework for human development and performance

Language

At the foundational level of the proposed framework, we have the language we use and the words we choose. Here, the language is viewed as a system of thoughts as described by Noam Chomsky. In this context, the avoidance of certain words is as important as the intentional use of others. The deliberate choice of words and language feeding into the engine, which is the left brain, generates thoughts, which are the bedrock of human transformation and achievement. Individuals, educators and leaders will benefit from cultivating a positive and empowering language in themselves and those under their care and leadership. You may have noticed that successful and optimistic people who positively impact others often use highly energetic and positive language. In the next chapter, we shall say more about the power of language when it comes to programming our minds.

Narrative and Stories

In his book *The 7 Habits of Highly Effective People* [2], author Stephen Covey tells a version of this story: One day, a man and his three young children walked into a train station. The children were very playful, and they went on annoying everyone at the station, endangering themselves as well as the other people. The father showed little interest in what the children were doing and did not attempt to restrain them. Seeing him as an irresponsible father, many people grew frustrated as the children continued their dangerous and annoying horseplay.

What went through your mind while you read the paragraph above? Did you sympathise with the busy commuters and share their frustration and concern for the safety of everyone, including the children?

If so, you are not alone but continue reading. Eventually, one commuter decided to intervene. The commuter approached the father and firmly told him, "Sir! Don't you think you should try to control your children? We all are trying to get to our destinations safely here!" The father looked confused and politely answered, "Yes. I guess you are right. I just don't know what to tell the children. I just came from the hospital, and their mother passed away a short while ago. I am truly sorry; I don't know what to do." Now, what is going on in your mind? If you are like most people, the frustration you felt earlier is replaced by feelings of sympathy, and there may even be guilt for jumping to the wrong conclusion without giving the man the benefit of the doubt. In both cases, you did not know all the details about what the man and his children were going through, and in both cases, your left brain filled in the blanks and told you a story that drove your emotions and even the behaviour of the commuter who approached the father. That is how powerful the stories we tell ourselves are.

During a training session that I delivered to the academic staff at my university, I asked the participants to share achievements that they could attain because someone else believed in them. Many inspiring stories were told, but I will always remember two stories shared by two colleagues. One of the lecturers shared that when she was a child, her father thought she was mentally disabled. He treated her as one, and she believed him! She was overwhelmed with emotions as she narrated that it was her mother, a lady who did not know how to read or write, who believed in her and told her that she could be whatever she wanted to be. The alternative story told by her mother propelled her to success. She ended up with a Ph.D. in mechanical engineering, which is not bad for a mentally disabled person!

Another lecturer said that when she was in primary school, she did not like school at all. She confessed that she used to put a storybook inside her schoolbooks and pretend to study while, in reality, she was reading her stories. One day, her teacher called her mother to give her feedback. Making sure that the child was listening, the teacher told the mother that her daughter had really beautiful handwriting. Our colleague said, "That statement totally changed my relationship with the school. I really wanted to impress my teacher." That same little girl now has a Ph.D. in chemical engineering.

We can never underestimate the impact of stories we tell ourselves about ourselves and others, how the world works on our success, and how we carry ourselves and manage our relationships with others. In the framework described here, the stories layer is right on top of the language layer. While the vocabulary we use and the language surrounding us power our stories, the evolution of these stories is not a simple process, as many parties contribute to directing them. This ranges from the media to our friends, parents and teachers.

When teachers teach their students about the world and encourage them to discover their purpose, pursue their dreams, achieve their full potential and learn how to live peacefully with others, these teachers are, in essence, trying to change and improve the stories their students are telling in their minds. When businesses or salespeople bombard us with advertisements in the media about their products and services, they want us to tell ourselves stories in which these products or services represent essential things for us. And when politicians campaign, they want to change our stories and adopt their political views as the way the world works.

Just like stories told in the minds of individuals, communities and organisations have their own stories, too. These stories are told through culture, folklore, legends and traditions, as well as vision and mission statements. The collective and common stories told by groups of people, especially large ones, are essential for these groups to work and operate effectively. In groups where people do not personally know each other, common narratives and shared stories about these groups that promote trust and a sense of identity and belonging represent an important social glue. In a nation, for example, very few know the president in person, but collectively, the nation tells a story about them and how they ascended to power. The same can be said about other national aspects, from economic and political systems to the constitution; they are the stories that groups of people opt to collectively tell, respect and accept as essential bases for national existence.

I recently purchased a microwave oven online. I did not know who sold it to me, but when I punched my credit card number, I trusted that the microwave would be delivered. Sure enough, I received the parcel in good condition in two days. Trust in the economic system emerges when enough people "believe" in it. It is a story that we tell together. We trust banks with our money because the story we all tell ourselves is that "when we want our money, the bank will give it back to us, plus interest." When this story is shaken, like what happened in Greece in 2015, when people started to have doubts about whether the banks would give them back their money, there was a run on the banks. The Greek government had to limit the daily amount of cash a depositor could withdraw from a bank, which made trust deteriorate even further. Whatever applies to nations can be used for other human groups, such as tribes, teams, schools and companies.

Awareness

We are not always aware of what is going on in our minds and the minds of those around us. That's why awareness of our stories, thoughts and feelings (self-awareness) and awareness of the stories, emotions and relationships around us (social awareness), represent an important link between the mental processes that take place in our mind and how our outlook is conveyed to the world.

The awareness layer is a very important one as it plays the role of a filter between the stories and the behaviour. Aware individuals, for example, will reject the language and narratives that dehumanise others, making stereotyping and ill-treatment of others more unlikely. Whether the negative language and narratives are self-generated or externally influenced, awareness of the stories told by individuals allows them the opportunity to edit and direct these stories in the most positive and productive way.

Regulation

Ultimately, the visible part of the human development and performance iceberg is our outlook and how we engage the world through the way we manage ourselves and our relationships. The roles that self-management and relationship management play in our success and happiness are well understood and cannot be underestimated.

It is to be noted that the awareness and regulation layers discussed above mimic the emotional intelligence framework developed by Daniel Goleman, and they will be discussed in detail later in the book within this context.

In summary, having more success, happiness and influence often requires a behavioural change on our part. As our behaviours, mindsets and habits are primarily driven by our internal narratives, a sustained behavioural change would mandate a transformation and shift in these internal narratives. The most potent way of shifting our narratives is by changing the language and words we use intentionally. Having an "Awareness" filter layer between the stories and the behaviour levels is an important feature that needs to be nurtured and strengthened.

The framework presented in this book integrates the language and narrative layers into the Daniel Goleman emotional intelligence framework with the aim of offering a comprehensive and enhanced model for change management, performance development and success. The different layers of the framework will be discussed further in the following chapters.

THE STORIES

We become the stories we tell ourselves. So we need to be careful what stories are we telling.

Our stories become our identities and realities, individual and organisational.

Research shows that there are

Groups who tell collective stories can work together and collaborate.

2 TYPES OF MINDSETS*

Our brains create a representation of the world inside them, we call these mindsets. Adopting a mindset is a choice.

These are team charters, organisational mission and visions and national values.

Fixed Mindset

Those with Fixed Mindset tell themselves a story about success being a result of innate capabilities that cannot be changed. When they fail, they get frustrated and give up.

CHOOSE THIS

Growth Mindset

Those who choose to adopt Growth Mindset tell themselves a story that success is governed by attitude and the willingness to put the necessary effort, rather than innate capabilities only. When they are faced with obstacles or when they fail, they view this as part of the learning and keep on trying."

*As described by CAROL DWECK

HUMAN DEVELOPMENT

A FRAMEWORK FOR INDIVIDUAL AND ORGANISATIONAL CHANGE

The language we use powers the stories we tell ourselves.

Through awareness of our language, stories and emotions we can manage ourselves and our relationships better. This can lead to success and happiness.

Sustainable Change & Human development & Motivation

REGULATION

SELF MANAGEMENT   RELATIONSHIP MANAGEMENT

AWARENESS

SELF AWARENESS   SOCIAL AWARENESS

NARRATIVE

THE STORIES WE TELL OURSELVES TO DESCRIBE:

1. OURSELVES
2. HOW THE WORLD WORKS

LANGUAGE

THE LANGUAGE WE USE (INDIVIDUAL AND/OR ORGANISATIONAL)

If we want a sustainable positive change and human development, we need to begin by changing the language we use, telling different stories and developing awareness as well as regulate ourselves and our relationships.

(This page is intentionally left blank)

3

How to Programme a Mind

"The limits of my language mean the limits of my world."

Ludwig Wittgenstein

Have you ever tried to watch a YouTube video only to be greeted by a pre-roll ad that you cannot skip immediately? YouTube makes money from advertisements by forcing you to watch the first 5 seconds of an ad, hoping you will remain interested in watching the rest. Most of us will wait impatiently to click the "Skip Ad" button, and this represents a significant challenge for advertising agencies. Ogilvy Cape Town is a South African advertising agency that decided to transform this challenge into an opportunity when they worked on a pre-roll ad for the Audi R8. The ad focuses on only one feature of the car: its ability to accelerate from 0 to 100 km/h in less than 3.5 seconds. The ad shows the car speeding up while the screen indicates both the speed and the time lapsed. Once the 100 km/h and 3.5-second marks are reached, the screen turns black with the message "You can skip the ad now." Thinking about it, this is a truly remarkable and memorable way to advertise the car. This was possible mainly because the ad creators were able to reframe the situation and tell a different story, seeing the limited time available as an opportunity rather than a challenge.

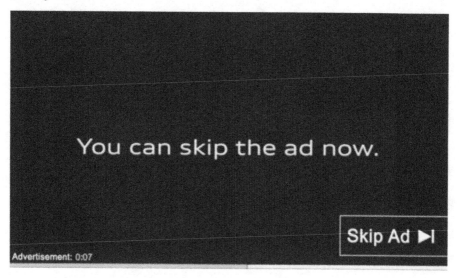

Gone in 5 Seconds: Audi R8 Ad

In the rest of this chapter, we will discuss how we can use language to systematically reframe situations positively and develop mental habits to tell more useful, motivating and compelling stories.

Language and Thinking

We mentioned earlier that Noam Chomsky postulated that language primarily evolved as a mode of creating, processing and interpreting thoughts. Interestingly, the development of A.I. is shedding a similar light on this topic as demonstrated by the success of Large Language Models (LLMs) generative A.I. (like ChatGPT and Google Bard) compared to A.I. systems that used to attempt to code a rule-based approach to intelligence. Modelling human language appears to resemble intelligence, further supporting the hypothesis that the language we use plays a direct role in programming our mindsets. We shall continue to explore and establish the relationship between language, thinking and the stories we tell. It is also interesting to note here that computer science research has contributed a fair share of our current understanding of how thinking in our minds takes place. Just like the case of the human brain, we use language to programme our computers. Computer programming languages are used to manipulate different variables in the computer programme. Before the computer can process a variable, the variable is required to be declared or named. This is like giving the variable a birth certificate and a location in the computer's memory. This process is followed by classifying the variable or stating its type. For example, a computer variable can be classified as real, integer or character. Once a variable is named and classified, the programme can process it. Several theories have been put forward to describe how thinking takes place; my favourite is the one that elucidates the role of language in the formation of thoughts. This theory is briefly described below and has implications for how we learn and communicate. Similar to computer programming, thinking and learning happen in three stages:

1. Naming (labelling)
2. Classifying
3. Processing

For the brain to store and process ideas, thoughts and concepts, it starts by assigning them names. We do that all the time; whenever we are faced with a novel situation or when we meet new people, the brain needs to give them names in order to store them in memory and eventually process them. If we meet someone and we do not know that person's name, we may use a feature of the person as a name. If the person is tall, we may name him "The Tall Man," if she is not from this country, we may name her "The Foreign Lady," and so on. This facilitates the storage part of the thinking. This naming stage is critical and is fuelled by the language we use. It will also have an impact on how the whole thinking process unfolds.

Now, if we are interested in a person, object or concept, our brain shall attach some classification to it. This classification could be anything such as: good, bad, hot, bitter, difficult, etc. In other words, a story is told about what we have just named to integrate the new knowledge or information into the existing narrative and make sense of the whole thing. This is achieved by electrochemical activity in the neurons (firing), which will result in initiating neuronal connections in the brain to process the new concept. The interesting thing about this theory is that it provides some control over the entire thinking process by altering the naming and classifying stages.

Let me illustrate this with an example that I use when I deliver my training sessions. When I show a picture of a cockroach and ask the audience to name it, they will all say it is a cockroach. So, this is the naming stage. When I ask them what they think of it, most say things like dirty, disgusting, ugly, etc. This is the classifying stage. This reflects the mental models and stories typically told about this creature, which is one of the international symbols of disgust. When the audience is asked what should be done with the cockroach, the majority will recommend destroying it because they are 'wired' to do so.

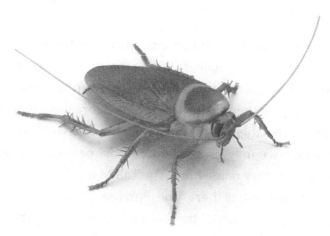

A cockroach

After explaining the thinking theory, I show the picture of the cockroach again and ask the audience to name it without using negative terms. This implies not using the word "cockroach", as it has many negative connotations already. One suggestion is to use its scientific name, *Blattaria*. This is a fresh name with no prior classification attached. Now, the audience is asked to describe the Blattaria using positive or neutral terms in order to invoke more positive stories. Sure enough, suggestions like 6-legged, brown, flyer, resourceful, flexible, protein-rich and even "roommate" start to emerge. When I ask, "What should we do with it?" an apparent shift in the mind of the audience is present, and they are not necessarily recommending destruction anymore. Suggestions such as using *Blattaria* as a source of protein or even installing sensors and cameras on it start to emerge. Using different naming and classifying terms creates new stories and brain patterns that are wired through training and repetition, and this is how learning takes place.

Using positive language at the naming stage can have an immediate impact on our capacity to develop new hopeful mental habits that can help us conceive solutions to the challenges we face and engage with the world more optimistically.

As a practical exercise, at the university where I was the dean of engineering, we outlawed using the P-word (problem) and replaced it wherever it appears in our language and the curriculum with the word "Opportunity." The same deal is made with everyone who takes my Massive Open Online Courses (MOOCs).

It is worth mentioning that shifting our language is never easy. When I personally began replacing the P-word with the word "Opportunity," I was surprised by how little control I had over the language I used. That is why I enlisted the help of people around me to monitor my language and point out when I used the P-word. We made an agreement that I would donate 1 Dollar to charity every time I used the P-word.

Inspired by the symbolism of paying 1 Dollar to charity when we fail short of honouring our pledge to shift our language, and to encourage our students and staff to stop using the P-word, we created what we call the "Opportunity Note." Modelled after a Dollar, I give each one of my students an Opportunity Note at the beginning of my courses; if they keep their promise of not using the P-word throughout the semester, I will personally sign the Opportunity Note for them. I have also mailed Opportunity Notes around the world to my online students. I do not have a way to watch my students 24/7, but creating a physical object (the Opportunity Note) makes the word come to life. As more students report empowering and enjoyable experiences, the stories and culture continue to take root. The Opportunity Note is shown below. I recommend that you remove the P-word from your vocabulary and begin to influence your stories and thinking process at the naming stage.

The Opportunity Note

Now, when I speak about using language to redirect our narrative and create a more positive mindset, I offer the audience the opportunity to have an Opportunity Note each and make a pledge not to use the P-word. This ritualises the whole process and creates an even more substantial impact. The pictures below show different groups taking the pledge.

Students from Dundee University and Heriot-Watt University posing with their Opportunity Notes

Deborah Ramirez, one of the MOOC participants, displayed her commitment to eradicating the P-word by putting a sign that reads "Say No to the P Word" on the rear windscreen of her car, turning heads and creating conversations around the role of positive language wherever she goes. We will read more about her story later in the book.

Several students in my Massive Open Online Course (MOOC) reported how using language to reframe their stories helped them in different contexts.

Humaira Ansari, a clinical hypnotherapist from Manchester, UK, commented that "Stripping off the P-word of its power by replacing it with the word 'Opportunity' has been one of the most useful methods

I use with my clients, helping them unlock their unlimited potential within and overcome any stuck-ness they may experience."

Medical Students from the National University Malaysia (UKM) pledging not to use the P-word

Say no to the P-word

Asma Harb from San Francisco, USA, said, "Replacing the 'P-word' with the word 'Opportunity' has made magic in my life! I have become a more focused, more organised and more determined person with the brilliant thought in my mind that I can make a real change and always challenge any obstacle and problem I face and turn them into new opportunities!"

Ferial Fakier, a participant from Australia, said, "I am a healthcare practitioner, practising for seven years before I joined a global healthcare equipment company in sales and marketing. There is almost a natural tendency to be negative in an environment where income is driven by sales, meeting targets and extended hours of travel. After challenging myself to exclude the P-word from my daily vocabulary, constantly adjusting my mindset to be positive, and proactively acknowledging my emotions, my colleagues have noticed a change in me.

"I then started noticing a boomerang effect on my team and the people around me; the positive energy I was giving off was now constantly bouncing back at me. I liked this!

"I then challenged the team I work with to exclude the P-word from their vocabulary; it was now some game we were playing. We have incorporated words like solutions, pivot points, and obstacles. Some people have given it a whole new, humorous perspective. I recall some colleagues using 'My situation needs healing' and 'we can Band-Aid that'.

"This concept in my team is still at the teething phase, but I've already seen some positive changes in the team, a point where we all are committed to thinking of positive outcomes and assessing our emotions towards challenging situations," Ferial concluded.

Lao Tzu once said, "Watch your thoughts; they become words. Watch your words; they become actions. Watch your actions; they become habits. Watch your habits; they become character. Watch your character; it becomes your destiny."

It is worth noting that in some languages, like Arabic, there are two different words to represent the English word "problem", "Mushkilah" is the Arabic word for problem as a source of trouble or worry, and "Masaalah" is the translation of problem as a question raised for intellectual or philosophical enquiry. Replacing the word "problem" with "opportunity" is aimed at creating mental habits of seeing all problems as solutions in disguise that require unearthing and discovering.

Knocking a man out with one punch, also referred to as a "king hit," was causing an increasing number of casualties in Australia. In July 2012, a "king hit" caused the death of Thomas Kelly. Another victim, Daniel Christie, was in a critical condition after receiving a "king hit" on New Year's Eve of 2014. This has sparked a debate about using the term "king hit," which seems to glorify violence. Some activists, together with the family of Daniel Christie, are suggesting to change the term from a "king hit" to a "coward's punch." This renaming is meant to deprive this act of violence of the glory that its current name lends. Mike Gallacher, the NSW State Police Minister, agreed with this proposal and encouraged the community and media to use the term "coward's punch" instead to help embarrass and shame offenders.

Words represent the materials of our thoughts. For us to be able to intellectually engage objects, persons, behaviours or phenomena, they will need to have names that describe them first. For example, a relatively new paradox is that individuals grow more disconnected from those physically close to them as the world gets more connected. This is exemplified by behaviours that are still new that they do not have names attached to them, such as ignoring the person in front of you in favour of your smartphone. Perhaps this lack of naming is the reason why we are not able to address this challenge effectively. In

May 2012, a group of people were determined to change this. They gathered at the University of Sydney in Australia, and among them was a lexicologist, a phonetician, a debating champion, a poet, authors and a cruciverbalist (a professional crossword maker). They suggested the word "phubbing" (a combination of phone and snubbing) to describe "the act of holding a mobile phone in a social setting of two or more people, and then interacting with that mobile phone and not the people in that setting." Now we have a word to describe the behaviour, and we can say things like "Stop phubbing me!" or "Don't be a phubber," or even "#SayNoToPhubbing."

We live in a world that is made of our words. People can make our day by saying a nice word to us, and, similarly, hearing a harsh word can spoil our moods for a long time. The thinking model of naming-classifying-processing is an invitation to cultivate a language that facilitates the realisation of opportunities as well as success, happiness, and potential fulfilment for everyone involved.

It is established that the human brain creates a representation of the world for us to process the world mentally. Stories play a central role in this representation, and renaming existing concepts in this representation can assist in reframing situations. Just like renaming a P-word as "Opportunity" or the cockroach as "Blattaria," if we would like to improve a relationship with a "Difficult" colleague, one way is to start by renaming that colleague, in our minds, so instead of calling them the "Difficult person," we may pick a trait of the person that is more positive and declare that as the new name.

It is necessary here to mention that renaming situations, people and objects to reframe situations and initiate positive development is not akin to encouraging people to be in denial. On the contrary, it is an active and creative approach to channel the energy positively towards creating a different reality.

In 2013, 34-year-old Alex Lewis led a normal life in Stockbridge in the UK. He ran his own business successfully until he contracted the streptococcal infection, a disease that resulted in the amputation of his arms, legs, nose and even lips. One could only imagine how difficult and distressing the situation was for Mr Lewis and his family. However, amazingly, Alex told the BBC, "The year I lost my limbs was the most brilliant of my life." He did not describe the year as "Difficult" or "Challenging" but "The most brilliant." By creating a positive narrative, Alex could cope better with what he was facing. He sure did not wish that he lost his limbs, but now that he is a quadriplegic amputee, he needs to make the best out of the deal. He opted to focus on the love and support that his family and friends offered him, as well as the fact that he was still alive and able to support his family. His positivity was a necessary ingredient in his recovery and rehabilitation. After fitting him with prosthetic legs, Alex started a 10-week walking course, but he surprised everybody as he walked again within two weeks.

The Brain, Learning and Mindset

Two bedridden, seriously ill men shared a room at a hospital. One had a bed closer to the only window in the room. Every afternoon, for an hour, the man was made to sit up to drain the fluid in his lungs. That is when he can peer through the window overlooking a beautiful park with a scenic lake. He can see children playing with their model boats and lovers walking while holding hands as the sun reflected over the surface of the lake as if it were a silver mirror. The man closer to the window kept describing what was happening in the park to his fellow patient, who was always looking forward to that time of the day when he learned what was happening in the world just outside the hospital. He closes his eyes and allows the visions of happiness and beauty to fill his mind. One day, there was a parade in the park, and while he was unable to hear the sound of the music, he listened to the vivid descriptions coming from his friend close to the window, and he was able to see the parade in all its detail. The days went by, and one day, the nurse bringing the morning medication was confronted by the man's lifeless body near the window. The body was removed, and the remaining patient indicated his interest in moving his bed closer to the window. His wish was granted. Once settled down, the man painfully sat up and looked through the window. To his surprise, he found that the window was facing just another wall! Puzzled, the man asked the nurse when the wall was erected and where is the park his late friend used to describe to him daily. The nurse was really surprised as she explained not only that the wall had always been there but that the dead friend was blind!

I bet that as you read the description of the lake and the park, just like the other man in the hospital, you could almost hear the music and see the sunlight reflected on the surface of the lake. As discussed earlier, the brain generates stories and mental models that impose order on chaos and deduce patterns to compare with previous experiences, impacting how we perceive ourselves and others and interpret the world around us. Faced with the same reality, different people have different mental models, and that is why we perceive the same events differently, drawing different meanings from them. For example, if two individuals are learning how to play the violin and both struggle equally with their learning, that struggle is nothing but an event happening to both of them as they push the limits of what they are capable of. Each individual will use their mental models to interpret this event (The Struggle). One mental model may be "playing the violin needs more practice; if I persevere long enough, I will be able to play beautiful musical pieces in due course". Another mental model may be, "This is difficult for me. I do not have the musical talent; I will never be able to learn how to play the violin." It is clear how each mental model will drive the individual harbouring it on a different path.

Decades of research in human motivation indicate that its primary source is our search for meaning. We are optimistic, motivated, resilient and on top of our game when we work on something meaningful to us. To achieve this state of sustained motivation, it is essential to work towards discovering and articulating our purpose and continue training and rewiring our brains to develop the muscles of positive thinking that are necessary to view challenges as opportunities so that we can, through them, create a better world.

The collection of mental models that we myelinate and cultivate result in our overall mindset and attitudes that drive how we perceive the world, our role in that world, and how we respond to the challenges we encounter. When confronted with a new situation, one individual may see adversity, while another may see opportunity, depending on the mental model they adopt.

Entrepreneurship, innovation and creativity are simply mental models that individuals adopt. Entrepreneurial, innovative, creative and highly motivated individuals cultivate the ability to generate positive mental models crafted to see opportunities in any new situation. Being able to see the opportunity even in adversity is synonymous with the ability to create positive and flexible mental models to see the world through.

Growth Mindset

In the book *Mindset*, Carol Dweck described two types of mindsets. The first she called "Fixed Mindset," which is held by individuals who believe that the capabilities that they have are fixed by their genes and their current circumstances. The second type is the "Growth Mindset", which reflects a narrative that describes capabilities and skills as things that can be learnt and developed, provided sufficient commitment and effort are dedicated to that. We can say that the mindset is the story we tell, and probably, you have guessed that those with a growth mindset are more capable of developing themselves and adding value to themselves and those around them. The role of leaders and educators is to encourage as many people as possible to adopt a growth mindset. [1]

Malcolm Gladwell studied many high-performing individuals in his book Outliers, including Bill Gates and Tiger Woods. He concluded that to achieve mastery level in a major competitive discipline such as sport, art, science or business, individuals need to dedicate around 10,000 hours of focused practice and training. This level of commitment and consistency is clearly an indication of the growth mindset. Whenever we see a master performing, we are tempted to think that the master is talented and lucky to be able to perform at that level. The fact of the matter is that mastery is always a product of a mindset that sees the struggle in new challenges as a stepping-stone towards progress and high performance. This is true for golf, chess, physics or music. All masters practice their craft religiously, building and strengthening myelin layers over the neurocircuits that they have cultivated over repeated and conscious practice. We are not saying here that talent or physical traits do not play a role. Undoubtedly, if you are taller than average, for example, you will have a better chance of excelling in basketball. The argument here is that more than talent is needed for mastery. [2]

To be successful in life and work, the ability to develop positive stories and mental models is paramount. Creating these positive stories and mental models requires committing the time and effort to practice and learn, necessitating many sacrifices on the way.

There is sufficient evidence that we can exert control over what habits, stories and mental models we form through repetition, reflection, willpower and intentional thinking, as well as the use of experienced coaches and mentors. These intentional mental activities cause myelin growth and strengthen the neuron connections, literally hardwiring the mental models we are inculcating. Through this, we are able to nurture positive mental models that will support growth, development and learning. The collections of mental models we maintain will create our world and form our mindset.

Nurturing positive growth-inclined stories and mindset is very necessary for success both professionally and in life at large. Individuals who continuously develop their mindsets and attitudes are lifelong learners who will be able to fulfil their full potential and play a key role in helping others achieve the same. In order to be effective individuals who can develop people, products and systems that make life worth living and support the increasing population of our planet, it is essential that we develop a positive attitude, see the world as full of opportunities and cultivate mental habits to construct mental models that enable us to spot those opportunities and create value out of them. Here, we must reiterate that our perception of reality is extremely important. Strictly speaking, there is no absolute reality, which is why two individuals facing the same situation may end up seeing adversity or opportunity depending on their mental model.

Studying the biographies of successful individuals who managed to have a lasting impact on those around them suggests the existence of a formula or a process for success. This formula seems to imply that success happens when we work on something we are interested in and willing to commit our time and effort towards. Interest and commitment, when coupled with the proper practising technique, coaching and feedback for improvement, will result in achieving mastery and success. These elements are discussed below.

Interest

The journey to success starts with interest. Successful people often pursue goals that they are interested in and are in alignment with their life purpose. Nudging life goals and the inner narratives towards each other will enable the left brain to continue weaving the coherent, meaningful story of our existence, allowing us to create meaning.

Simon Sinek calls this "start with why". In his book carrying the same title, he cited many examples of organisations and individuals from Martin Luther King to Apple Inc. where successful and inspirational leaders are very clear of the "why", the purpose for their existence, and use that to communicate and inspire. It is important for individuals and organisations that seek success, happiness and fulfilment to articulate their interests and life purpose, as this is the key to sustaining them throughout the ups and downs of the life journey. Writing down a "Purpose" statement for both individuals and organisations is a worthwhile effort in this direction. If done right, it can bring a lot of clarity to answer the existential question, "What is the purpose of our existence?" [3]

Commitment

Pursuing what interests us is an essential starting point, but more is needed for success. We need to be committed to allocating the time and effort necessary to build the success mindset. Willingness to push the limits and operate outside our comfort zone is a prerequisite for honing new skills and attitudes leading towards success. Interestingly, that willingness to explore uncharted territories is also the reason why we will inevitably face failure before we achieve mastery. This "failure" is a necessary feedback that we should use to know what to change and where to improve in order to fare better next time. The way we respond to failure is an excellent indication of the depth of our interest in what we are pursuing, and it represents a reflection of our mindsets and the stories we tell ourselves as well. It is necessary that we cultivate awareness of the story we tell ourselves when we are faced with difficulties so that we can nudge the story in a positive and helpful trajectory. An interested, committed mindset will perceive failure as getting us a step closer to success by uncovering shortcomings and identifying aspects that require change.

It is necessary here to mention that the definition of failure in this section, and most of the book, is the inability to achieve the desired results when we push the limit of what we are capable of or what the current paradigms allow. This failure often yields very positive learning that can be used to further improve performance in the future.

Practising Technique, Coaching and Feedback

Techniques are mental structures and templates we use to improve our performance while pursuing our developmental goals. Often, these techniques are used under the tutelage of a coach, teacher, mentor or a master of some sort. Techniques refer to the way sportswomen and sportsmen train when they prepare for the Olympics, for example. The presence of a coach is often very important. I taught myself swimming at the age of 27. I had the interest, and I was truly committed. I went to the swimming pool every day and watched how other people swam. Eventually, I was able to swim, but my technique was not good at all. I attribute this to the fact that I did not get someone to show me how to do it right and provide me with timely feedback so that I could correct and alter my technique and build myelin around the proper brain circuitry.

The practice that leads to success takes place with full awareness on the part of the trainee while a selected limit is being pushed. For example, when a runner tries to break their own record, they may try a new rhythm of running or breathing. As they try this new breathing technique, their performance may take a dip. They need to be aware of what is happening in their body and mind and continue practising, fine-tuning and perfecting the skill. When a limit is pushed, any failure is feedback or a symptom that indicates that further fine-tuning is necessary, so failure should be expected, accepted and even welcomed as a sign that we are on the path to enhancing and improving the skill.

How to Craft Habits and Mindsets

It is obvious now that the formation of mental models is a process that happens over time as myelin grows along the associated neuronal pathways. We have a choice of allowing this process to take place unconsciously or to take charge of it and literally use myelin to craft our desired mindset. This section proposes three main techniques for growing a positive mindset: brain rewiring, language and thinking as a mental model.

We mentioned earlier that mental models to recognise danger exist much earlier in the evolution of the brain as they can be a necessary prerequisite for survival. However, mental models that identify opportunities can be taught. One exercise that can be used to improve our capability to see the positive side of events is Brain Rewiring. This is where we purposefully record five things we are grateful for daily. Students who took my courses were required to perform brain rewiring daily. By the end of the semester, most of them reported increased capability to see opportunities in their lives. The following chapters dedicated to emotional intelligence will discuss this in more detail.

Change Management

The framework described in this book can also inform and guide transformation and change management processes. The goal of change management is often to transform and change behaviour at an individual, team, organisational, national or even global level. This may take the shape of becoming more health conscious (individual), communicating openly (team), becoming more customer-focused (organisation), transforming the educational system (national), or even reversing climate change (global). Time after time, change management efforts fall short of achieving their targets because they focus on changing the behaviour through extrinsic motivations without transforming the inner language and the narrative.

A more sustainable approach to change management happens when the strategies adopted to enact the desirable change are orchestrated at all levels, starting with language, introducing new narratives and developing awareness of that narrative leading towards the more desirable behaviour, which can be supported with a reward scheme.

Simon Sinek, the bestselling author of *Start with Why*, said that he felt nervous when he first started speaking to large audiences. Noticing that the body reacts in similar ways when nervous and when excited, Simon began to tell himself that he was excited before he went on stage. This made a massive difference in the way he behaved and delivered his highly acclaimed presentations.

The same can be said when transforming businesses, organisations and even nations. While redirecting the use of resources, information, business processes, and budgetary allocations is very important to organisational change management, a sustainable change should be accompanied, if not led, by a shift in organisational language and narrative—more about this in the coming chapters.

(This page is intentionally left blank)

4

Success and Emotional Intelligence

"If your emotional abilities aren't in hand, if you don't have self-awareness, if you are not able to manage your distressing emotions, if you can't have empathy and have effective relationships, then no matter how smart you are, you are not going to get very far."

Daniel Goleman

"We cannot tell what may happen to us in the strange medley of life. But we can decide what happens in us, how we can take it, what we do with it, and that is what really counts in the end."

Joseph Fort Newton

Humans are the most successful species on earth. For better or worse, we control the world we live in. There exist a number of explanations as to why we are more successful than other animals. However, the author of *Sapiens*, Yuval Harari, attributes this success to our ability to collaborate flexibly in large numbers. While a large number collaborative behaviour is exhibited by other species, such as ants and bees, the collaboration demonstrated by these species is rigid and limited in context. "If a beehive is facing a new threat or a new opportunity, the bees cannot reinvent their social system overnight in order to cope better. They cannot, for example, execute the queen and establish a republic." Harari said [1]. Other species may hunt collaboratively, which requires working flexibly together, but this often happens in small, tightly-knit groups of blood-related animals like a pride of lions. The main reason behind this unique human success is our ability to tell and believe collective stories about our teams, tribes, organisations and nations. When we collectively believe in our economic, legal, and political systems, we can collaborate with those with the same belief, even if we do not know them in person. We can trade and exchange services because we believe that we will be paid for our work and that the money we will receive is accepted by others when we want to exchange it for what we want. We also believe that banks will give us back our money upon request, and when our rights are breached, we can go to the authorities and ask for help.

So clearly, at more levels than one, our success depends on our ability to build relationships, trust each other and work collaboratively in large groups. The quality of the relationships that we are in does not only determine how successful we are. It determines how happy and healthy we are, too. In our interconnected world today, the notion of relationship extends to our relationships with our environment and our responsibility to other species.

Emotional intelligence starts with self-awareness, which is the awareness of our own emotions, existence and our role in the bigger scheme of things, as well as our impact on our surroundings and others. Emotional Intelligence extends to how we can build successful and thriving relationships with others. In a nutshell, possessing high levels of emotional intelligence results in nurturing good relationships with others, including our loved ones, customers, work colleagues, superiors and even the natural environment we exist within, and this will inevitably make us happy, healthy and prosperous.

Recently, the concept of emotional intelligence began to attract the attention of educationalists, business leaders and policymakers. There is a huge opportunity to integrate emotional intelligence systematically into the education system so that individuals are given the opportunity to develop these essential skills through a holistic education. Holistic education and human development are integrated processes that aim not only at developing skills necessary for employment but also at ensuring the emotional wellbeing of individuals. This often is referred to as training the head, heart, and hands. The good news is that the only part of the body that we need to train is the brain. Knowledge, emotions and even manual skills are all cultivated, developed and stored in the brain. The integrated, holistic development of knowledge, skills, and emotional competencies will result in individuals who are not only ready for employment but also ready for life's challenges through being resilient, purpose-driven individuals who can fulfil their full human potential and help others achieve the same. Purpose-driven individuals have a positive growth mindset that gives them a belief that they can positively impact life. This motivation is a necessary prerequisite for approaching work and life optimistically.

While the emotional intelligence sections of this book draw on the writings of Daniel Goleman, especially *Emotional Intelligence* [2] and *Working with Emotional Intelligence* [3], these sections are not intended as a replacement for reading Goleman's excellent books. In fact, I highly recommend them. As mentioned earlier, I taught a free Massive Open Online Course (MOOC) called *Success with Emotional Intelligence* to more than 5,000 students. Participants from all over the world found the tools I introduced useful and complemented the theoretical framework described by Daniel Goleman.

I measured the emotional intelligence of the students who attended my course and compared it to that of a control group. The measurement happened twice, at the beginning of the semester, when the course was offered, and at the end of it. To infer the level of their emotional intelligence, students were asked to complete a detailed questionnaire. The results were very encouraging, with the students who completed the 18-week course achieving growth in all aspects of emotional intelligence compared to the control group. In this chapter, I will attempt to introduce the concept of emotional intelligence from a big-picture point of view to prepare us for a more detailed examination over the following chapters.

What is Intelligence?

Intelligence is a widely used word, but we seldom stop and ask ourselves what it means. It has been defined in a variety of ways that are related to cognitive capacities in humans. Intelligence has been observed in nature and other living creatures as well. Artificial Intelligence is the capacity that is programmed into machines (computers), enabling them to respond to new situations and learn. Intelligence can refer to the mental ability to think, learn, recognise patterns, logically predict outcomes, and respond to a variety of stimuli. Steven Pinker, the author of *How the Mind Works*, defines intelligence as the ability to attain goals in the face of obstacles by means of decisions based on rational (truth-obeying) rules. Intelligence Quotient (IQ) is the measure of the ability to comprehend logical, geometrical, and mathematical challenges [4]. While IQ is a useful indication of future success, the challenges of the 21st century increasingly need other kinds of intelligence that IQ does not measure. Historically, what made humans special, when compared to other creatures and even intelligent machines, is their high intelligence and consciousness.

Interestingly, the last few decades resulted in the creation of highly intelligent machines that were able to beat humans at the game of intelligence. On 11 May 1997, Deep Blue, a chess-playing computer designed by IBM, defeated Gary Kasparov, the chess world champion. Since then, more and more machines are getting better at doing intelligent work that used to be considered exclusively in the human domain. The latest in this series was ChatGPT, the Large Language Model generative A.I. that was released in November 2022, which is capable of conversing impressively with humans responding to a wide range of knowledge and creativity challenges. In all likelihood, this trend will continue, and it will significantly impact the nature of work that humans will be doing. With more jobs being automated and being done by machines, we need to cultivate skills and mindsets that will allow us to remain relevant in the world.

Interestingly, with all the progress made with machine intelligence, very little advancement happened in the realm of artificial consciousness. As consciousness and the emotional domains remain strictly human-centred, perhaps these will be the areas to focus on to future-proof ourselves as technological developments change how we live. This will go hand in hand with developing higher-order thinking skills.

As explained in the previous chapters, the brain has three main regions: the old brain, which is dedicated to survival instincts; the middle brain, where emotions are processed; and the new brain, where rational high-level thinking happens. We perceive the world around us through the variety of sensory signals that are relayed to our brains. Signals flow in and out of the brain through its lower parts, the old and middle brains, which means that any signal that goes through the brain will be emotionally "flavoured" before reaching the new brain for rational processing. This is the reason we sometimes emotionally overreact to events and stimuli. Being aware of this emotional overdrive and being able to manage the impact of emotions on ourselves as well as others around us is called Emotional Intelligence.

Surviving and thriving in the 21st century, which is a key century that is riddled with Grand Challenges for humanity as a whole, requires the holistic development of individuals in both the cognitive and emotional domains. This is a prerequisite for nations' competitiveness, prosperity and security. Despite the broad realisation that national education systems ought to be geared towards providing holistic education, there is a gap between this realisation and what happens in reality at schools and universities around the world. In his book, The *Global Achievement Gap*, Tony Wagner identified 7 survival skills for the 21st century that are not systematically developed in schools today [5]. These skills are:

1. Critical thinking
2. Collaboration across networks
3. Agility and adaptability
4. Initiative and entrepreneurialism
5. Effective oral and written communication
6. Accessing and analysing information
7. Curiosity and imagination

It is clear that to maintain nations' competitiveness and achieve holistic development of individuals and societies, it is paramount to adopt an integrated approach to inculcating both IQ and Emotional Intelligence, leading towards developing human capital equipped with all the necessary survival skills.

Emotional Intelligence

Deep inside our hearts (or, shall I say, brains), we are all ultimately chasing happiness. We may be seeking success in the form of money or power, or we may be seeking status or fulfilment, but if we dig deeper, often happiness is what we find as our fundamental motive. Happiness is not easily defined either, as it means different things to different people. The definition I like is that happiness is the quality of one's relationships. If you think about it, after achieving the basics in life, such as having health, food and shelter, what really matters is how good our relationships with our loved ones, students, teachers, co-workers, fellow drivers on the road, and almost everyone else. Collaboration and teamwork, which are vital success skills in today's work, school, and life in general, are also functions of the quality of relationships that we are able to cultivate and develop with others. Emotional intelligence is an essential ingredient for nurturing healthy and productive relationships. It is the skill and ability to understand, recognise, predict and appropriately respond to emotions in oneself and others, as well as in groups and teams. Daniel Goleman presented a neat and helpful framework to describe the four aspects of emotional intelligence, namely self-awareness, social awareness, self-management and relationship management [2]. The framework, together with a description of its main elements, is discussed further in the following chapters.

It is clear that Goleman's emotional intelligence framework sits within the broader framework of human development and performance described in Chapter 2, which has four layers: the language, the narratives, the awareness and the regulation. The last two layers are the emotional intelligence part.

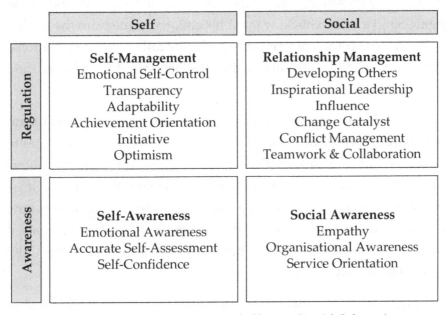

Emotional Intelligence Framework. (Source: Daniel Goleman)

The Business Case for Emotional Intelligence

Besides achieving wellbeing and health, which are no trivial things to attain, scientific evidence points towards the finding that emotional intelligence is good for businesses' bottom line. Coupled with the widely accepted view that it is possible to develop and improve one's emotional intelligence skills through training, intentional use of language and positive habits inculcation, this should be good news. Businesses and organisations worldwide, from the US Air Force to L'Oreal, are seeing the benefits of either recruiting emotionally intelligent individuals or even supporting the development of emotional intelligence traits within their people.

Happiness Index

Not only businesses are recognising the importance of emotional intelligence, wellbeing and happiness, but nations too. As a matter of fact, the Kingdom of Bhutan was ahead of the game in recognising the importance of promoting and measuring happiness earlier than many corporate players. Bhutan is a small country in the Himalayas. While nations traditionally measure their progress and performance using the Gross Domestic Product (GDP), the former king of Bhutan, King Jigme Singye Wangchuck, wanted his country to measure the quality of life in more complete terms using what he called the Gross National Happiness (GNH), striking a balance between the spiritual and material needs.

In 2013, on a planning retreat with the senior management team of the university I worked for, we were asked to develop strategies to be implemented to improve the experience of our various stakeholders. Inspired by the GNH, I proposed to create the GIHI (Gross Institutional Happiness Index), a composite index that measures how balanced our experience is. To add a dramatic effect, I also proposed that we rename the VC (Vice Chancellor) of the university the CHO (Chief Happiness Officer).

GNH of Bhutan measures nine domains that can be adapted to educational institutions and other organisations, as shown in the table below. We started collecting the data to create our GIHI, and interestingly, a few months into the process, the Star newspaper quoted the Second Finance Minister of Malaysia, Datuk Seri Ahmad Husni Mohamad Hanadzlah, saying, "For decades, the progress of the nation has been popularly measured by the Gross Domestic Product

(GDP). However, the GDP is inadequate to measure the nation's wellbeing, and a new approach to measure wellbeing effectively is required." He said this in his opening remarks before chairing the 2014 Budget Focus Group Meeting on *Developing a Malaysian Happiness Index: Work-Life Balance*.

Academic institutions have a unique opportunity to lead society in promoting holistic human development, which is a pressing need in this complex and rapidly changing world we are living in.

Domains of the Gross National (and Institutional) Happiness Index

	GNHI	GIHI
1	Psychological wellbeing	Emotional wellbeing
2	Health	Health and Safety
3	Time use	Time use
4	Education	Learning and Staff and students Development
5	Cultural diversity and resilience	Cultural diversity and resilience
6	Good governance	Good governance
7	Community vitality	Building flourishing communities
8	Ecological diversity and resilience	Campus sustainability
9	Living standards	Compensation and Benefits

In February 2016, the United Arab Emirates appointed a "Minister of Happiness" to show the government's commitment to promoting happiness and life satisfaction amongst the residents of the state. "Happiness is a serious job for governments," said Ohood Al Roumi, the UAE's Minister of Happiness. "The main job of the government is to create happiness. In 2011, the UN encouraged the member countries to look at happiness for a holistic approach to development. The role of the government is to create an environment where people can flourish – can reach their potential – and choose to be happy." She told the CNN news channel.

The government of UAE has recently selected 60 officers from different government departments to undergo intense training in the science of happiness at leading mindfulness and positive psychology centres in the UK and USA in order to prepare them to implement the necessary policies in the happiness domain.

Not to be surpassed by Bhutan and UAE, Madhya Pradesh became the first state in India to set up a "Happiness Department" in July 2016, with Chief Minister Shivraj Singh Chouhan heading the department at its inception stage. It will work to ensure "happiness in the lives of common people" along the lines of Bhutan. The Happiness Department organised a happiness week where villagers in the state participated in games and other activities aimed at raising their levels of happiness and satisfaction.

The United Nations has adopted the 20th of March as the annual World Happiness Day, and it now publishes an annual report entitled the World Happiness Report. The report rates the happiness levels in 142 countries. In 2023, Finland ranked number 1 for the 6th consecutive year, and Afghanistan took the bottom rank of 142 [6]. The Happiness Index is a composite of various factors such as GDP per capita, social support, healthy life expectancy, freedom to make life choices, generosity, and perceptions of corruption.

To be part of this movement, educational institutions must acknowledge their role in fostering emotional wellbeing, positive behaviours and attitudes among learners, in addition to imparting knowledge and skills.

While the concept is straightforward, it's important not to conflate simplicity with ease. Constructing an educational system centred around producing impactful graduates is an inherently challenging endeavour. This aspiration necessitates the creation of an entire community dedicated to nurturing student growth and furnishing personalised developmental experiences. The emphasis should be on nurturing purpose-driven, emotionally intelligent, resilient, and content graduates.

At Heriot-Watt University Malaysia, we pursue this goal through a series of initiatives, including the HappierU programme (where "U" signifies both "You" and "University"). This university-wide effort aligns the community with psychologist Vanessa King's 10 Keys for happier living: Giving, Relating, Exercising, Awareness, Trying-out, Direction, Resilience, Emotions, Acceptance, and Meaning (forming the acronym GREAT DREAM) [7]. The underlying principle is to portray happiness as an attainable state through practical actions. For instance, during a blood donation drive, we're reminded that both Giving and Trying-out (for those donating blood for the first time) can elicit feelings of satisfaction, joy, and happiness. HappierU is intended to build a flourishing community of students and staff where everyone is supported by and being supportive of others so that we can all achieve our full potential. This is not the sole provenance of academics; HappierU is led by students and staff from both in and out of the classroom. Human Resources, Campus Services, Careers Advisors and Counsellors all play a crucial role in delivering our goals, which we measure with a Happiness Index.

Whether at an individual, organisational or national level, happiness and emotional wellbeing are increasingly seen as serious business that needs to be approached scientifically and systematically. The coming chapters will outline specific approaches and techniques that individuals and organisations can utilise to develop and grow various aspects of emotional intelligence.

	SELF	**SOCIAL-RELATIONAL**
REGULATION	**SELF MANAGEMENT** Emotional Self Control Transparency Adaptability Achievement Orientation Initiative	**RELATIONSHIP MANAGEMENT** Developing Others Inspirational Leadership Influence Change Catalyst Conflict Management Teamwork and Collaboration
AWARENESS	**SELF AWARENESS** Emotional Awareness Accurate Self Assessment Self Motivation Self Confidence	**SOCIAL AWARENESS** Empathy Organisational Awareness Service Orientation

5

Self-Awareness

"And you? When will you begin that long journey into yourself?"

Rumi

"Self-awareness is our capacity to stand apart from ourselves and examine our thinking, our motives, our history, our scripts, our actions, and our habits and tendencies."

Stephen Covey

In 2010, Green Peak Partners and Cornell's School of Industrial and Labour Relations conducted a study to examine the role of business executives' interpersonal traits in the success of achieving overall business objectives. The study examined 72 executives at public and private companies with annual revenues from $50 million to $5 billion. While the research examined several executive interpersonal qualities, self-awareness seems to stand out as a prognosticator of success. The search to fill leadership roles gives short shrift to self-awareness, which should actually be a top criterion. Interestingly, a high self-awareness score was the strongest predictor of overall success. This is not altogether surprising as executives aware of their weaknesses are often better able to hire subordinates who perform well in categories in which the leader lacks acumen. These leaders are also more able to entertain the thought that someone on their team may have an even better idea than their own [1].

The starting point and the cornerstone of emotional intelligence is self-awareness. It represents awareness of the stories we tell ourselves about who we are, what is happening within us, and our strengths, weaknesses and limitations. Emotionally intelligent individuals are aware of their internal state, capabilities and limitations, and they are not only able to use language to describe how they feel in clear and precise words, but they can select the language that can positively impact how they and others feel. These individuals can manage themselves better and can develop better relationships. Through awareness of what drives and motivates them, self-aware individuals are able to pursue aspirational and challenging goals that they manage to continue to chase, even if the obstacles are numerous, mainly because they have a clear sense of purpose.

According to Daniel Goleman, self-awareness encompasses emotional awareness, accurate self-assessment and self-confidence. This chapter will unpack this further and provide some suggested exercises to develop self-awareness.

Emotional Awareness

Emotions are often what sets us in motion, and the basis of emotional intelligence is to be aware of our own feelings and emotions and to be able to describe and express them accurately. This is easier said than done, though. One of the reasons for this is that the middle brain, where emotions are processed, is incapable of processing language. Try to ask people how they feel. I bet the answer will be words like "fine", "ok" or something along these lines. Being aware of our emotional state is the first step in cultivating emotional intelligence, and developing the language to describe our emotional state is a prerequisite for achieving emotional awareness.

To help the students who registered for my online emotional intelligence course develop the language to describe their emotions, I requested that they report their emotional and relational states daily using specific adjectives in 6 different domains, namely Mental, Emotional, Relational, Spiritual, Vocational, and Physical domains. I learned this framework from Jim Warner, who coaches top executives and CEOs around the world, and he starts his forum sessions with a "check-in" where everyone reports their M.E.R.S.V.P. state.

The process of reporting one's emotions daily was difficult initially, and the students found it almost agonising as they forced themselves to describe their emotions. As time went by, the process got easier and more enjoyable. Throughout the process, I assured the students that "all emotions are okay." The purpose of the exercise was to create awareness of our feelings and not to deny them or suppress them. Below is a sample of how course participants report their feelings daily.

My Emotions Today. Participants reported how they felt daily, creating more self-awareness

As you can see from the example above, often, the M.E.R.S.V.P. domain reporting starts some discussions on the nature of the state of each domain. This sharpens the awareness and creates a sense of community. You can do this exercise in a number of ways. You may join the online course and perform the exercise with the other participants, or you may report your daily emotions in your diary or even write them on a board at home, work or school. To help with the description of the feeling in each domain, the table below contains a suggested list of adjectives to choose from.

Sample adjectives that can be used to describe how we feel.

Domain	Definition	Sample adjectives
Mental	Mind, intellect	thinking, sharp, focused, curious, open, blocked, challenged, questioning, confused, learning, growing, wondering
Emotional	Affective state of consciousness	happy, sad, fearful, disgusted, guilty, confused, aware, excited, satisfied, loved
Relational	Quality/state of relationships	connected, grounded, networked, blessed, separated, reaching out, supported, lost, misunderstood, betrayed
Spiritual	Bigger cause/meaning	blessed, grounded, assured, doubtful, searching, enlightened, driven, betrayed, disappointed, fulfilled
Vocational	Job, career or study	progressing, stuck, challenged, stretched, supported, driven, focused, confused, realistic
Physical	Body and health	healthy, strong, in pain, flourishing, recovering, refreshed, healing, renewing

Accurate Self-Assessment

For us to progress in life, it is essential to know our strengths, weaknesses, opportunities and threats. We also need to recognise that, at times, our strengths and weaknesses or even our opportunities and challenges are hidden in a blind spot that we are unable to see, and we may need the help of others to shed some light on them. There exists a number of tools to approach accurate self-assessment. The following are two of them.

SWOT Analysis

SWOT analysis is a reflection tool to explore Strengths, Weaknesses, Opportunities and Threats (Challenges). Performing a SWOT analysis can profoundly impact our accurate self-assessment and self-awareness. Strengths are positive internal qualities and capabilities an individual (or an organisation) has. These can be physical traits, skills or character qualities that can help achieve goals. On the other hand, weaknesses are internal shortcomings that need to be addressed further to ensure the achievement of objectives. Opportunities and threats represent external events and circumstances that can potentially be useful or harmful.

	Self	Social
Benefit	Strengths	Opportunities
Harm	Weaknesses (Areas for Growth)	Threats (Challenges)

SWOT Analysis

As we perform the SWOT analysis, we can have a more accurate self-assessment, allowing us to capitalise on our strengths, use our weaknesses as opportunities for growth and be ready to grab opportunities, and face challenges.

Johari Window

Johari window is a self-discovery graphical tool created by psychologists Joseph Luft and Harrington Ingham in 1955, hence its name. It is used to help people better understand their relationship with themselves and others. It is basically a two by two matrix resulting in 4 quadrants containing what you know and do not know about yourself, as well as what others know and do not know about you. This is shown in the following figure.

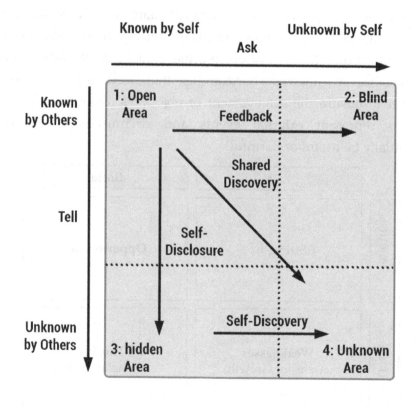

Johari Window

The four quadrants are discussed briefly below:

1. Quadrant 1 (Open Area): This contains your visible behaviours, qualifications, attitudes and values that both you and those around you recognise that you possess.

2. Quadrant 2 (Blind Area): These are things that others see in you that you are unaware of. Think of it as something that is smeared on your face. While you do not know of its existence, others see it clearly. This includes both physical and psychological aspects and can be either positive or negative. Examples of physical blind spots include body odour and the annoying repetitive use of some words during speech. Deeper blind spots may refer to the feelings of unworthiness and inadequacy that some of us may carry without being aware of. Positive blind spots are mainly associated with our potential. A tall person, for example, may often be seen as someone who can do well in basketball, even though that person may not have considered playing the sport.

3. Quadrant 3 (Hidden Area): This area includes things known to you but hidden from others. This may include personal history, personal connections and health-related matters.

4. Quadrant 4 (Unknown Areas): Things that are unknown both to yourself and others and represent an excellent domain for discovery and exploration.

The Johari window can be used to achieve a number of objectives, including knowing more about ourselves and bringing our team members closer to each other. In both cases, the aim is usually to widen the open area horizontally (by asking for feedback) and vertically by revealing things to others. In the process, some discoveries in the unknown area may happen, improving self-awareness.

In a team building setup, team members may construct their own Johari windows on large flipcharts, put some descriptions in both the open area and the hidden area, then everyone sticks their window on the wall, and the attendees go around and provide feedback in the blind area. It is worth mentioning here that it is vital to pay attention to the social and cultural context when giving feedback and when revealing things about oneself. Some societies are more open than others when giving and receiving feedback. Trust needs to be established, too, to ensure that nothing that is revealed will be used against the individual who reveals it.

Self-Confidence

The American Psychological Association (APA) Dictionary defines self-confidence as "trust in one's abilities, capacities, and judgment." As you can imagine, nurturing this self-trust is a lifelong dynamic process that requires learning, effort and practice. We also need to recognise that the levels of self-confidence can vary throughout our life journeys. For example, when we start a new job, join a new school, receive a promotion or find ourselves in unfamiliar situations, experiencing some degree of self-doubt is a natural response. It is well established now that self-confidence is a skill that can be practised and improved. Below are specific strategies that can be used to enhance self-confidence:

1. Use positive and affirming language when speaking to yourself and when describing yourself. The foundation of this book is that the language we use will shape our attitudes, including how much we trust ourselves. Many people find public speaking, for example, difficult and stressful. They may tell themselves, and sometimes even others, a version of this statement: "I am not good at public speaking." An alternative, and more empowering, narrative could be, "Public speaking is challenging for me, but if I train long enough and invest sufficient effort in this, I can improve my public speaking skills." The second script is not only more empowering, it can help conquer the inner critic which is a significant step towards building self-confidence.

2. Cultivate self-awareness. Gaining awareness of one's current state along the 6 M.E.R.S.V.P. domains and conducting realistic self-assessment will enable a picture of an individual's strengths and potential as well as limitations to emerge. Playing to strengths and viewing the limitations as areas for improvement, individuals (and even organisations) can improve their abilities to tackle challenges as they come along.

3. Define your purpose. Having a clear sense of purpose and what brings meaning to your life and having definitive plans to mobilise this purpose into a positive impact on the world represent significant sources of inspiration, motivation and self-confidence.

4. Be prepared. Trust is established over time through a consistent track record. This principle applies similarly to self-trust. When facing upcoming tasks, whether an exam, a job interview, or a business presentation, ensure thorough preparation. Accumulating small victories and leveraging them can significantly contribute to the enhancement of self-confidence.

5. Push your limits. Challenging yourself, mentally or physically, through setting ambitious SMART goals can be a strategic way to improve your capabilities and foster more self-reliance. Furthermore, intentionally subjecting yourself to uncomfortable situations will train you to handle these situations more adeptly in the future.

6. Keep on learning. The world is changing rapidly, and keeping current knowledge in our fields of interest and speciality can provide us with an essential source of self-confidence.

7. Stay connected. The personal and professional networks that we belong to can be an important source of help, affirmation and knowledge. Staying connected with those who believe in us and are interested in our success is a wise strategy.

8. Look your best. The way we look impacts how others perceive us and even how we perceive ourselves. Being well-groomed and dressing professionally can contribute towards feeling more confident.

9. Maintain the correct body posture. A 2009 research study [2] conducted by Richard Petty and his colleagues from Ohio State University, published in the European Journal of Social Psychology, unveiled that individuals who maintain an upright posture while recording their thoughts exhibit enhanced confidence in these thoughts.

In their remarkable experiment, two groups of students were tasked with jotting down their top three positive or negative personal traits, either in an upright or slouched posture. Following this exercise, the students evaluated their anticipated future professional performance through a survey. The outcomes were striking. Those who sustained an upright and confident posture displayed a significantly greater alignment between their self-ratings and the traits they had documented compared to students adopting a slouched and less confident posture.

Richard Petty, who is a psychology professor, highlighted that these findings underscore the impact of body posture, not solely on external perceptions but also on self-perception, telling the Science Daily, "The results show how our body posture can affect not only what others think about us, but also how we think about ourselves."

A growing body of evidence suggests that our sensory and motor systems are more connected to our cognitive processes than we think. This is called embodied cognition, and it can be a powerful tool in influencing our mood, confidence level, and emotional state in general. For example, if we are feeling down, a suggested exercise would be to tilt our heads and look up at the ceiling or the sky. Doing that for 30 seconds can give us a positive boost. As the saying goes, it is difficult to feel down when looking up. Amy Cuddy performed research on power posing, and she showed that individuals who practice power poses, such as extending their arms up in a V shape while opening up their chests or laying their hands on their waists (like Wonder Woman), for only 2 minutes experience an increase of testosterone (dominance hormone) levels of about 20% and a decrease of cortisol (stress hormone) levels of about 25%. These changes are real and often lead to positive performance in stressful and demanding situations, such as job interviews. Designing a virtuous cycle in which we use our body postures to positively influence our emotional state will improve our productivity and performance in a manner that can make the positive change more permanent. Amy Cuddy said: "Don't fake it till you make it. Fake it till you become it." Embodied cognition will be referenced again in the book when we discuss techniques to improve self-management.

10. Practice self-care. Foster your physical and mental well-being through nurturing healthy practices like consuming nutritious food, exercising regularly, ensuring adequate sleep, and incorporating meditation into your routine.

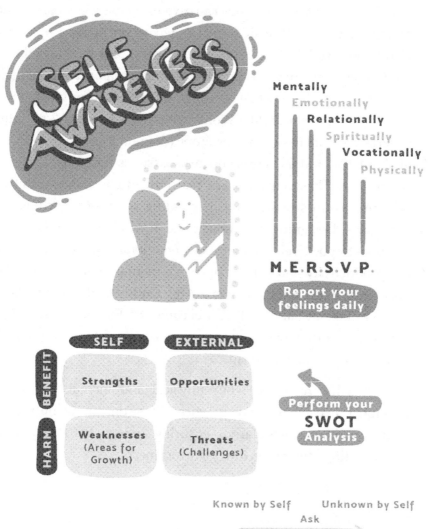

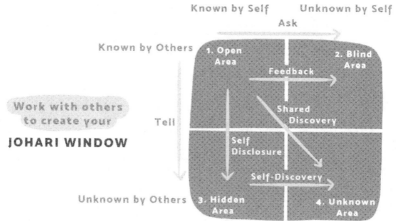

6

Social-Awareness

"Opinion is really the lowest form of human knowledge. It requires no accountability, no understanding. The highest form of knowledge is empathy, for it requires us to suspend our egos and live in another's world. It requires profound purpose and larger-than-the-self kind of understanding."

Bill Bullard

"The bigger triangle is bullying the smaller one. The circle hides, but the bigger triangle tries to disturb it, and the smaller triangle rushes to help." This is what my 10-year-old son said when I showed him a short animation that was developed by Fritz Heider depicting two triangles and a circle moving around. The bigger triangle follows the smaller one. It looks like it's pushing it around. My son is hardly alone in seeing drama, emotions, intentions and feelings in what should have been two triangles and a circle moving around in a two-dimensional space. As a matter of fact, almost everyone who watched the short animation had a similar reaction. Human minds have the innate capacity to perceive others in terms of their intentional mental processes. We are always interested to know what others are thinking about and how they feel about it. This is called the Theory of Mind (ToM), and this capacity is hardwired into us and is the basis for our social life.

Just like self-awareness, social awareness refers to the presence of the mind and other character traits that enable individuals to be aware of their surroundings and how they are impacted by and impact other people's feelings and emotions. To nurture social awareness, Daniel Goleman proposed the development of empathy, organisational awareness and service orientation.

Empathy

Empathy is the ability to put ourselves in the position of others and feel how they feel. It does not necessarily mean to agree with others, just to feel what they feel. This is extremely necessary for all social animals, and it has its roots in the biology of the brain. Italian researchers discovered specific neurons in the brain that are activated not only when we go through an experience but also when we see someone going through a similar experience. That is why, for example, if we see someone accidentally hitting her finger with a hammer, we can almost feel the pain in our fingers. These neurons are now dubbed "mirror neurons."

Empathy is a very powerful capability, and those who cultivate it can be good team players. Empathy is essential for professional success as well. Engineers and designers, for example, need to develop empathy with the end users of their products so that they can develop human-centric designs.

Studies of the history of malpractice litigation against doctors revealed that empathetic doctors who exhibited care and listened well to their patients were at a much lower risk of being sued for malpractice by their patients when something went wrong compared to doctors who were perceived as less empathetic. Empathy is also a key skill for those who work in sales, marketing and customer service.

One practical way to develop empathy in product design is to use the product through a process that is called "bodystorming." Imagine a group of male engineers tasked with designing a car being pitched to female customers. Suppose the future customers are expected to drive the car while wearing high heels and carrying handbags. In that case, the bodystorming entails the male engineers putting on high heels, carrying bags and trying to get into the car and drive it. Not only imagining the experience but literally going through it. The knowledge acquired through bodystorming is very valuable and often profoundly influences the design process. After turning forty, I started to have challenges reading fine print. This includes the numbers and letters on my TV remote control as well as some business cards. Although I think that, at times, the fine print is made fine on purpose to fool consumers, in the case of my TV remote control and name cards, the designers are either young or used enlarged models of their design on their computer screens. In both cases, putting themselves in the shoes of different age groups of their end users would have significantly improved the design.

When my colleagues who are new to teaching ask me how to know if the time allocated for their final exam papers is sufficient, my advice is to choose a quiet corner and answer the exam paper as if they are sitting for it themselves and time the exercise. The time allocated for the students should be 1.5 times the time the lecturer needs to complete the paper.

To develop empathetic skills, students in my *Success with Emotional Intelligence* course on campus were grouped in pairs. Each of the two students was asked to describe their feelings while the partner listened empathetically and non-judgmentally. The partner then reciprocates and listens back. After that exchange, each partner narrates the feelings of their partner back to them.

Dining in the Dark is a restaurant series started in 1999 to give sighted customers the experience of eating as a blind person. The restaurant is made pitch black, while the food is served by blind or visually impaired individuals. The restaurant aims to enable sighted people to empathise with blind people by being in their shoes for a short period. This also leads to more appreciation of the ability to see, an ability many of us take for granted.

In general, we can develop empathy by adopting an attitude of trying to see the world from others' points of view, actively working towards validating the opposing point of view (rather than just rejecting it outright), listening to the other's points of view and accepting to disagree.

Organisational Awareness

Organisational awareness refers to the ability to sense the dynamics of a group of people or team. This includes at which stage the team is in its growth cycle as well as the centres of power, such as who calls the shots and who may be playing a negative role in the team. More will be shared about the team's growth cycle in the coming chapters. Organisational awareness allows the individual to gauge the level of emotions in a group as well as how this can be positively influenced.

Having organisational awareness is an important skill to acquire and develop in order to achieve professional success.

Service Orientation

Service leadership is being recognised as a sustainable leadership style. Leadership is influence, and servant leaders can command the respect of others and have a positive influence over them, enabling their teams to achieve their goals. To develop service orientation, it is important to get involved in activities that go beyond the direct benefit of an individual and have a positive impact on others. Through serving others, we can develop a sense of self-worth and usefulness while building our capacity to understand the plight of those around us. Gradually, service learning is being acknowledged as a viable development technique for building emotional intelligence traits in students.

John-Son Oei is a passionate young man. After graduating with a degree in communication, he was searching for his life purpose and inner calling. "I chose to study communication because I thought it was a generic degree that would help me find what I should be doing later in life. However, after graduating, I was even more confused." John-Son told my students while delivering a guest lecture as part of one of my MOOCs (Massive Open Online Courses). While enjoying life and making money modelling, John-Son wanted to do something more meaningful.

Travelling one day with his friends, he visited a village of one of the Malaysian indigenous people groups (called *Orang Asli* in Malay), and he was shocked to know that some of them did not have a proper home to stay in. He was particularly disturbed seeing a broken shack with a man living there. Something inside him made him feel that he should act. He set up a Facebook event inviting his friends to join him to build this man a house. He was surprised by how many people were willing to help. They spent a weekend building the house and even gave it a paint job. Encouraged by what a group of untrained but enthusiastic people can do, John-Son went on and founded EPIC (Extraordinary People Impacting Community). This social enterprise seeks to create a cooperative world with "response-able" people driven by a heart for service. Through EPIC, the movement of EPIC Homes, an initiative that aims to provide homes for the *Orang Asli*, began.

EPIC Homes has a very interesting business model. It converts the home-building exercise into a team-building challenge that clients, such as companies and organisations, can perform over three days. The client will pay for the materials needed to build the house, plus the experience and EPIC Homes will supervise the client's team throughout the home-building process. The home is then presented to the identified *Orang Asli* family. This service learning exercise is a very interesting and innovative initiative that EPIC Homes is pioneering.

The partnership takes place between the beneficiary family and the team that is building the home. "Poverty is a state of mind," John-Son says. "In order to empower the family that will receive the home, EPIC engages the village to determine the selection process and the family members in the design of their future home. They can choose from a range of designs that not just fit their land practically but their personal taste too. They are also given a choice of orientation, special layout and what colour the paint will be," he added.

To ensure that the beneficiary family does not see the house as a free hand-out, the family members are also required to participate in building their house and also to pay it forward and help build two other homes with their neighbours. This had a very interesting spillover; as members of the *Orang Asli* community participate in building their homes, they develop handy skills that have helped some of them gain employment. This has led to many empowered beneficiaries who have gone on to help other families, even outside their own village, getting involved in disaster recovery efforts outside their own state as not just builders but trainers, leaders and positive role models of service leadership to other beneficiaries. EPIC Homes has built over 200 homes thus far, a small dent in the 12,000 homes needed by the *Orang Asli* community in Peninsular Malaysia, according to John-Son.

I was honoured to be part of the team that built a home for Juri, Masni and their three children. Taylor's University, where I worked back then, sponsored the project. The senior management team of the university, supervised by the EPIC Homes team, worked very hard to build a nice and simple house in three days.

The work EPIC does is an excellent example of service orientation. Service orientation is an important and necessary trait to develop social awareness through feeling the needs of others and being able to play a positive role in fulfilling these needs. We can all develop our service orientation by giving to others, helping people in our communities, volunteering and supporting worthy causes.

John-Son Oei, Founder & CEO of EPIC

Building a Home for Masni and Juri (Mushtak Al-Atabi)

Develop empathy with others by

PUTTING YOURSELF IN THE SHOES OF OTHERS

 Try to SEE the world from others point of view

 VALIDATE the other point of view

 LISTEN and accept to disagree

BE OF SERVICE TO OTHERS

Volunteer

Give others

Support a worthy cause

Help people in your community

7

Self-Management

"Mastering others is strength. Mastering yourself is true power."

Lao Tzu

"The first and best victory is to conquer self."

Plato

In the 1960s, Walter Mischel and his colleagues performed a series of experiments with the pre-schoolers at Stanford University's Bing Nursery School. The test setup was straightforward, a child was asked to sit in a room and was presented with two choices: to have a tasty treat (for example, a marshmallow) right away or have two marshmallows if the child was willing and able to wait for around 20 minutes. As expected, some children were able to delay gratification and resist the temptation to enjoy the bigger reward, while others did not hesitate to eat the single marshmallow. Mischel, a psychologist, was studying the dynamics of delayed gratification and self-control among children. However, his research resulted in some interesting insights. In a follow-up study on the same children more than a decade later, researchers found that those who were able to exert more self-control as children had better academic performance, earned more money and were even fitter than those who were unable to exercise self-control. In his book *The Marshmallow Test*, Mischel examined willpower and whether it can be taught and developed. His research showed that willpower is a skill that can be cultivated, and this is indeed great news. [1]

No matter how we define success—a happy family, robust health, fulfilling career, financial independence and self-actualisation—it seems to be associated with both intelligence and emotional intelligence, particularly self-management. We have established that emotional intelligence is the one domain that we can influence and improve. Managing self is an essential component of emotional intelligence and a strong indicator of success in life. Individuals who are aware of their own emotions and their surroundings learn that all emotions are okay. It is okay to be angry, sad or happy. However, not all actions are okay, and while they cannot control what life may throw at them, they can choose the way they respond. They realise that it is not acceptable, for example, to insult others or physically harm them while they are angry or disappointed.

We will always be exposed to external events and stimuli as we go through the ups and downs of life. Angry motorists will shout at us, co-workers will misunderstand us, and people will cut the queue ahead of us. We need to accept that we will never be able to control external events that happen to us. What we have control over, however, is how to respond to these events, and this is called self-management. Viktor Frankl, author of *Man Search for Meaning*, said, "Everything can be taken from a man but one thing: the last of human freedoms - to choose one's attitude in any given set of circumstances, to choose one's own way." An angry motorist can push our buttons, and this would surely make us angry and frustrated, but we can still choose the way to respond to this stressful situation. We can smile and even apologise to diffuse the confrontation or shout back and escalate the situation to a fight. [2]

To survive in the environment in which our ancestors lived, our brains evolved to respond quickly to negative stimuli and threats. If a caveperson is walking in the jungle, it makes sense for them to run if they feel danger approaching rather than stopping and analysing the consequences. This fast action that served us well in the past has become a liability that we need to mitigate in today's world. There is a need to train our brains to be able to identify and quickly respond to opportunities, not only threats. This fits clearly in the realm of self-management.

The Willpower Muscle

In one of the most famous experiments in psychology, Roy Baumeister asked a group of students to fast for several hours before getting them into a room where they were allowed to eat. The aroma of freshly baked chocolate chip cookies filled the air and the hearts of the hungry students with anticipation. As you may expect in a psychological experiment, there was a twist. The students were randomly assigned to eat the cookies or plain raw radish. The researchers left the students alone with both the cookies and radish within their reach, simply to maximise temptation. Watching from a hidden window, the researchers observed those assigned to eat radishes wrestling with the temptation. Some took the cookies in their hands and smelled them, savouring their fresh scent. To their credit, none of those assigned to the radish succumbed to the lure of eating the forbidden food. This set the stage for the final part of the experiment, where all the students, including a third control group that was asked to fast but was offered no food, were told that they would be tested for cleverness using sets of puzzles. The puzzles, in fact, were unsolvable, and the real aim was to see how long the students would persevere before giving up.

On average, students who ate the cookies spent 20 minutes attempting the puzzle before giving up. A similar time was scored by the control group. Interestingly, the radish group gave up after only 8 minutes on average. This is considered a very significant difference.

This experiment was replicated by research groups around the world in different settings but with similar results. Willpower seems to be akin to a muscle that gets fatigued when strained. Those who spent their willpower resisting the cookies had little left in their reservoir to resist giving up on the puzzles. Interestingly, just like muscle, willpower can be trained and exercised to be stronger in order for us to have better self-control [3].

This leads to a simple and logical conclusion: One of the most effective ways to develop self-control is to avoid the depletion of the willpower reservoir through avoiding temptation. For example, if you wish to start a dieting programme, make sure that you do not have snacks that are easily accessible between meals, or even better, remove all the snacks away from your home. During the marshmallow test, children who were able to wait the whole 20 minutes avoided temptation by distracting themselves by singing, examining the furniture in the room and avoiding looking at the forbidden treat.

According to Daniel Goleman, self-management entails emotional self-control, transparency, adaptability, achievement orientation, initiative and optimism. The following section describes the various techniques and activities that can be used to improve self-management. I introduced some of these techniques during my Massive Open Online Course to help cultivate different aspects of self-management. Students found these techniques and activities to be beneficial and even life-changing.

Brain Rewiring

During the Korean War (1950-1953), the Chinese used what they called "lenient policy" to operate prisoner-of-war (POW) camps under their supervision. Unlike the North Korean POW camps that featured physical brutality and harsh punishment, the Chinese utilised a more psychologically focused approach to nudge captured American soldiers into submission and compliance to give military information, turn in fellow prisoners, and publicly denounce their country. The Chinese approach was so successful in getting the American POWs to collaborate with the enemy that it led to an extensive investigation by American psychologists after the war. These psychologists quizzed the returning POWs intensively to determine what had happened and how the Chinese managed to get them to inform on one another, a behaviour that was not prevalent among the American POWs in World War II.

While American servicemen were trained to provide nothing but name, rank, and serial number when captured, the Chinese captors used their keen understanding of psychology to subdue their captives. They would, for example, ask a POW to make simple, seemingly inconsequential statements that were critical of the United States or were sympathetic to the communists. They will ask the POWs to agree to statements such as "the United States is not perfect" or "in communist countries, the government ensures that everyone has a job." They will then ask the POW to write these statements and sign his name to them. Slowly but surely, the Chinese ensured that the Americans were committed to their "statements" by broadcasting them to the rest of the camp. Ultimately, this changes the image of a POW of himself. He now sees himself as a collaborator.

I hope that this pattern is clear and recognisable to you by now. The Chinese were using language to alter the narratives (stories) of the POWs. The experience of American POWs during the Korean War shows us how making statements and affirming them over time can result in changing how individuals view themselves in their own narrative, leading to behaviours consistent with the new story. This realisation can also be used for good, for example, to develop a positive and optimistic view of oneself and the world. As repeatedly mentioned, the human brain seems hardwired to respond to negative stimuli. This trait was essential to ensure survival in the dangerous environment that our ancestors used to inhabit. However, this inherited asset may become a liability when it comes to situations where positive thinking and the ability to respond to opportunities are paramount. The good news is that the brain can be "rewired" to respond to positive stimuli.

One technique proposed by Tal Ben-Shahar in his book *Happiness* to achieve this is to keep a gratitude journal reporting things that an individual is grateful for daily [4]. I have institutionalised this exercise in my *Success with Emotional Intelligence* course, where all my students were required to report, in writing, five things that they were grateful for on a daily basis for the period of 18 weeks. Just like reporting the inner state daily, the *Brain Rewiring* exercise started as being awkward and challenging, as it required different brain muscles to be exercised and activated. With time, the exercise became more fluent, easy and enjoyable. At the end of the course, students reported a more positive perspective towards life and appreciated themselves and those around them more. This positive mental attitude is extremely powerful when addressing challenges, and it can cultivate the creation of innovative alternatives in both professional and personal life, as well as foster emotional self-control and optimism. Repeating this daily exercise for the period of the course was aimed at creating positive thinking attributes and literally building myelin along the mental circuits that enable us to see the goodness in situations and people. An example of *Brain Rewiring* is shown below.

Towards the end of the course, Susan, one of my online students, reported the following as one of the things that she was grateful for on January 11, 2014: "a really difficult conversation which brain rewiring enabled me to turn into a relationship building opportunity rather than a confrontation! Yeah!"

Another very interesting method to rewire the brain was reported by Mauricio Estrella. He shared this in his TED talk and a few online articles. After falling in love with a beautiful young lady and quickly getting married, things did not work out as planned, and the marriage ended in divorce.

Grateful for
Surving the day at work
Taking my daughter, for a bit, to work, which made her happy
Friends coming over tonight
The support I receive
Exercising! It really helps me tremendously to cope with stress

↳ Reply ███████████████ and 1 other like this Unlike

Absolutely awesome!
You made a memory today with your daughter that she will always remember!
Good job on the exercise!
Stay awesome friend!

↳ Reply   You like this Unlike

Brain Rewiring performed daily by the course participants

Times were challenging, and Mauricio was having difficulties letting go and moving on with his life. One day, he was rushing to a meeting and needed some files from his computer; starting his computer, he was confronted with a message telling him that his password had expired and he needed to set up a new one. The ICT policy of the company he worked for required that employees change their passwords monthly for security reasons. Frustrated as he was, he had a brilliant idea, "What if I use a password that will encourage me and cheer me up?" His new password was "Forgive@h3r." "My password became the indicator. My password reminded me that I shouldn't let myself be a victim of my recent breakup and that I'm strong enough to do something about it," Mauricio wrote in an article in the Huffington Post. Encouraged by how much this simple action helped him to accept what happened and move on, he went on to try new passwords to achieve different objectives. Below is a list that he shared in the same article.

Password	Result
Forgive@her	(To Mauricio's ex-wife). It worked
Quit@smoking4ever	It worked
Save4trip@thailand	It worked
Eat2times@day	It did not work
Sleep@before12	It worked
Ask@her4date	It worked. Mauricio fell in love again
No@drinking2months	It worked
Get@c4t!	It worked. Mauricio has a beautiful cat
Facetime2mom@sunday	It worked. Mauricio talks with his mom every week

"I still wait very anxiously each month so I can change my password into something that I need to get done. Remember, for added security, try to be a bit more complex with the words. Add symbols or numbers, or scramble a bit at the beginning or the ending of your password string. S4f3ty_f1rst!" Mauricio added [5].

As mentioned earlier, brain activities governing behaviour, habits, learning and thought expressions occur as electrochemical signals generated and transmitted along neurons. Neurons in the brain are widely connected, and that makes the electrical signals leak as they move along this complex network of wires. Performing tasks repeatedly and intentionally, such as *Brain Rewiring*, will get the brain cells firing signals in a particular repetitive fashion. Continuous firing stimulates the formation of the electrically insulating myelin sheath that encloses the path of the electrical signal. The more the neurons fire along the same pathway, the thicker the myelin layer and the better the insulation. In time, this will improve the strength and the speed of the electrical signals, which is how we get better at things after practising them.

The Plexiglas Concept

The Plexiglas Concept is a simple and powerful self-management technique. It can be used in both social and professional settings. Imagine if someone is accusing you of something terrible and untrue; your natural response is to feel under attack and start defending yourself, questioning the motives of the person attacking you. This often leads to escalation; usually, nothing good comes out of the situation. Next time you are emotionally attacked, imagine a thick, strong sheet of Plexiglas standing between you and the attacker. Imagine what you are attacked with is a physical object, a rotten fruit, for example. Now, as the attacker throws the object (insult, accusation) at you, you can see them, and as the thrown object hits the Plexiglas, it splatters, allowing you to see its content.

From your safety behind your Plexiglas, you look at the attacker and the object and say to yourself curiously, "How interesting!" This will allow you time to think and retell the story of what has just happened before responding. As the attacking projectile thrown at you gets smashed, metaphorically, on your trusted Plexiglas, you will get to examine its contents closely, allowing you the opportunity to further understand the attack and the attacker. There will definitely be some negative content, such as envy, hatred and misunderstanding, but there will also be some useful feedback too. Best of all, once you use the Plexiglas to allow you to delay your response, you can use the time to select the response that you prefer for that situation.

Purpose, Vision and Mission

A strong and, if done right, effective, story editing tool is having well-defined and compelling purpose, vision and mission statements. They help motivate us, draw our attention to the bigger picture and encourage others to support us and join our cause. These days, most organisations have these statements crafted and displayed on their walls. When done meaningfully and correctly, the vision and mission can provide a powerful tool to outline and communicate an organisation's or individual's purpose and core values. Compelling vision and mission statements are attempts to describe the purpose or "why" the individual (or organisation) exists.

Daniel Pink, the author of *Drive: The surprising truth about what motivates us*, outlines that, ultimately what motivates us is the pursuit of mastery, autonomy and purpose. Mastery results from our aspiration to get better at what matters to us, which leads to better skills. Autonomy is about having a choice to be self-directed in pursuing what we enjoy and find fulfilment in. Purpose is the desire to work on something meaningful that goes beyond one's self. William Damon, a Stanford University professor, defines purpose as "a stable and generalised intention to accomplish something that is at once meaningful to the self and consequential to the world beyond the self." A growing body of research is pointing towards the centrality of developing a sense of purpose as a prerequisite for mental health, success and happiness. In order for us, individuals and organisations alike, to explore our purpose and how it sits together with other essential things in life, the Japanese concept of ikigai, shown in the Venn diagram below, is instructive and helpful. It shows purpose at the intersection of doing what you love, what you are great at, what the world needs, and what you will be paid for [6]. While articulating purpose may look simple (in the diagram), it is not easy at all. It often takes effort, intention and reflection. It is, however, an investment that will pay a good dividend, particularly when A.I. is disrupting the world and humans need to be aware of what differentiates their offerings from what machines can provide. Furthermore, having a clear sense of purpose will enable individuals and groups to remain anchored, motivated and hopeful when things are challenging and uncertain. A well-articulated purpose has a convening power and can attract like-minded individuals to work together towards the greater good.

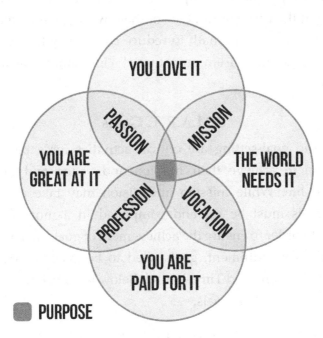

Identifying your purpose (ikigai)

A powerful and inspirational way to express a sense of purpose, vision and mission is by articulating an Impact Statement. This statement has three parts: the "I am statement," the "Purpose Statement," and the "Actions Statement." At my university, new students reflect on how they want to make the world a better place through their work, talents and the programme of study they choose. Coming up with an impact statement is never easy, and it takes a lot of one-to-one interactions with our academics. However, we found that the effort and time invested in writing an impact statement at the beginning of a student's first semester pays multiple dividends. Students who are aware of why they started studying are more likely to stay the course when the going gets tough.

When we ask students why they join our Actuarial Science programme, for example, they often say that they love mathematics and that having a degree in actuarial science will secure them a good job. After completing the impact statement exercise, students are clearer about their true north. One of them wrote, "I am a math lover. I will use my mastery of math to reduce complexity for others when they need it the most. I am an actuary." How is that for an Impact Statement?

S.M.A.R.T. Goals

Planning and goal-setting are critical activities for a person or an organisation to achieve their mission and vision and bring their purpose to life. While mission and vision may take a lifetime to achieve, goals must be set and completed in a more foreseeable timescale. In order to ensure the achievement of goals that accumulate towards mission fulfilment, goals need to be Specific, Measurable, Attainable, Relevant, and Time-bound. Below is a quick review of each aspect of the S.M.A.R.T. goals.

Specific Goals

A specific goal is clear and not ambiguous. It needs to indicate who is involved in achieving it, what needs to be accomplished, where it will take place, when it will happen and how it will be achieved. For example, "to get in shape" is rather a general goal, while "join a gym and work out three times a week for a minimum of 1 hour at a time" is a specific goal.

Measurable Goals

Here, we need to specify the metrics for measuring the goal so that we can unambiguously know when the goal is achieved. For example, "increase sales" is not measurable, while "increase sales by 10% compared to last year" is measurable.

Attainable Goals

For goals to be attainable, there should be no ethical or legal barrier against them. When setting goals, one must also acknowledge environmental and physical limitations. For goals to motivate, they need to represent a stretch on what is perceived as being possible while simultaneously ensuring that the skills, capabilities and attitudes that make the goals attainable are within the reach of those who are working on them. For example, if I do not know how to swim now, setting a goal of winning an Olympic medal in 6 months is unrealistic and may demotivate me as I go about my weekly training. However, the goal of qualifying for a local swimming competition within a year is very motivating; even though it stretches me, if I train long enough, I have a very good shot at achieving it.

Relevant Goals

The goals we set should be relevant and congruent with the overall purpose, mission and objectives of the team or the organisation. A football coach, for example, may set the goal of "making two egg sandwiches by 9 a.m.". The goal is specific, measurable, attainable and time-bound, but it is hardly relevant if the overall objective is to increase the tactical skills of the team. Relevant goals are worthwhile; they add real value and capitalise on the strengths and capabilities of the team members.

Time-Bound Goals

The goals need to have clear timelines indicating when they will be achieved.

While setting S.M.A.R.T. goals is a very important activity, it is essential here to remain flexible, agile and open to review the goals should an attractive unforeseen opportunity arise or when the internal or external environments change. If we work in the mining business and while digging for silver, we find gold; we should have the mental agility to change our goals to capture the new "golden" opportunity.

When I worked on my Ph.D. research, my project focused on exploring the relationship between fluid mechanics and the formation of gallstones in the gallbladder. The work involved building models of the cystic ducts of patients who underwent surgical removal of the gallbladder and studying the flow inside them. While observing the flow structures, I noticed that there was some fluid mixing occurring within the cystic duct that connects the gallbladder to the rest of the biliary system. While, strictly speaking, my S.M.A.R.T. goal was to explore the relationship between gallstones and the mechanics of the flow, I opted to pursue the mixing opportunity as a viable industrial option. This ended up being a significant part of my doctorate work and even influenced the title of my thesis, which I changed to *Cystic Duct to Static Mixer: A Serendipitous Journey*.

Let me iterate again: setting S.M.A.R.T. goals is crucial for successful planning. However, maintaining an open mind and preserving intellectual agility allows us to adjust the S.M.A.R.T. goals to yield the best outcome should there be a change that was not foreseen when the goal was set. When we change and update our S.M.A.R.T. goals, it is necessary that we communicate the change and its reasons to other team members and also document the change process adequately.

Smile, and the World Will Smile with You

When you're smilin'.... keep on smilin'
The whole world smiles with you
And when you're laughin'.... keep on laughin'
The sun comes shinin' through
But when you're cryin'.... you bring on the rain
So stop your frownin'....be happy again
Cause when you're smilin'.... keep on smilin'
The whole world smiles with you"

The above are the lyrics of one of Louis Armstrong's songs [7], which may prove true in more ways than one. While the common perception is that emotions precede facial expression, we feel happy, and then we smile, or we feel sad, and then we frown; scientific evidence is now pointing towards a more complex feedback loop between facial expressions and emotions. When you smile, you can start a chain reaction that will end up with you feeling better and happier, and by the same token, frowning can make you sad.

Paul Ekman, one of the leading authorities on emotions and facial expressions, was performing experiments with his colleagues on their faces to identify the facial muscles associated with different emotions. They used electrodes to stimulate these muscles and individually activate them. When they stimulated the muscles controlling frowns, they were surprised that they felt rather miserable at the end of the working day. This led them to hypothesise that activating specific muscles through smiling and frowning can generate the corresponding emotions [8]. A number of experiments have since confirmed this.

Recently, research performed by psychologists at the University of Cardiff in Wales suggested that individuals who received Botox facial treatment, which inhibited the muscles associated with frowning, making it difficult to frown, reported being happier and less anxious on average compared to a control group that did not receive

111

Botox treatment. The researchers corrected for the feeling of attractiveness among the studied individuals to ensure that the emotional improvement is not related to the psychological boost associated with the cosmetic treatment [9].

Earlier, when discussing self-confidence, we explored the role of embodied cognition in helping us cultivate a more confident mindset. The use of our facial expressions to help regulate our emotional state can be categorised as a form of embodied cognition, too.

We still need to fully understand the mechanisms by which our facial expressions affect our emotions and moods. However, what is sure is that when we smile, we can impact our mood positively, and the opposite is correct when we frown. So "keep on smilin."

SELF MANAGEMENT

Everyday report the

things that you are grateful for

All emotions are ok but not all actions are ok.

When emptions rise, be aware of them but delay your action so that you do not do anything that you may regret.

PLEXIGLAS TECHNIQUE

When you feel that you are emotionally attacked, imagine a strong Plexiglas is shielding you. Watch the attack splatter on your Plexiglas and say "how interesting!"

Identify **YOUR PURPOSE** and write your **MISSION AND VISION STATEMENT**

Set S.M.A.R.T. goals

Specific
Measurable
Attainable
Relevant
Time-bound

YOU LOVE IT

PASSION   MISSION

YOU ARE GREAT AT IT

THE WORLD NEEDS IT

PROFESSION   VOCATION

YOU ARE PAID FOR IT

(This page is intentionally left blank)

8

Relationship Management

"Relationships are all there is. Everything in the universe only exists because it is in relationship to everything else. Nothing exists in isolation. We have to stop pretending we are individuals that can go it alone."

Margaret Wheatley

"What keeps us happy and healthy as we go through life?" With this question, the psychiatrist Robert Waldinger started his TED talk in November 2015. In a recent survey of millennials that Wadlinger cited, over 80% of the respondents said that getting rich was their major life goal. Another 50% of these same young adults said that another major life goal was to become famous. Robert Waldinger is not an ordinary man. He is the director of a 75-year-old Harvard study on adult development, which is one of the most comprehensive longitudinal studies in history. The study was commissioned in 1938 with 724 men both from Harvard College and Boston's poorest neighbourhoods. Participants in the study are contacted annually and asked questions about their work, home life and health. When Waldinger delivered his TED talk, 60 of the initial participants were still participating in the study [1].

The finding of the study was simple: "Good relationships keep us happier and healthier." This sounds simple enough, and at a certain level, it feels expected, so how on earth so many people are thinking of money and fame as their major goals in life? Shouldn't we all spend more time and effort cultivating great relationships with our loved ones and with our communities at large? What leadership failure resulted in this situation? And more importantly, what kind of social, educational and political leadership is necessary to enable individuals and communities to achieve their potential and live successful, balanced and happy lives?

The research done in the areas of human happiness, motivation and success in the past two decades is pointing in the direction of having a sense of purpose, cultivating emotional intelligence and nurturing successful relationships as the bedrock for how individuals and communities remain motivated, resilient, happy and connected.

The question of happiness and how to achieve it is one of the essential questions that humanity spent centuries trying to find an answer to. Often, what we think will make us happy loses its appeal soon after we achieve or possess it. Understanding what keeps us happy, healthy, motivated and satisfied in today's world is a pressing need as we live in a highly complex and interconnected world where the stakes are very high. This has significant implications for education, family life, and the business world.

While self-awareness is the cornerstone of emotional intelligence, relationship management is its ultimate objective. As mentioned earlier, happiness is measured by the quality of relationships that we cultivate with those around us. The pillars of the character of an individual who is capable of nurturing and managing great relationships with others include being able to develop others, inspirational leadership, influence, being a change catalyst, conflict management, as well as teamwork and collaboration. These traits are discussed below.

Developing Others

A distinct sign of emotionally intelligent individuals and leaders is a genuine interest in developing others. An exercise we did to teach the skill of developing others in the students who took my *Success with Emotional Intelligence* course on campus was to pair students together and get them to interview each other to document each other's mission, vision, SWOT analysis and a SMART goal to be achieved by the end of the semester. Each student was encouraged to conduct the interview with care and respect and carefully write down their partner's mission, vision, SWOT and SMART goal.

At the end of the exercise, each student would have to face their partner and say their name followed by "Your SMART goal is _____, and I know that you will achieve it." Students are also asked to send each other specific encouraging messages related to their SMART goals twice a week. This can be done verbally, using email, text messages or even with a card. After completing the exercise, one of my students posted the following on the course website:

"Today, I would like to share something I should've shared a few weeks ago. During one of the lectures, we conducted an activity called mission partnership. I was hoping to be paired up with my best friend. But eventually, I was paired up with another person. A student from Kazakhstan named Ben (not his real name). At first, I dreaded it and thought I would fail the activity due to his lack of English communication skills and his 'blur'ness. But after starting the activity, my eyes were opened. I could see from his perspective. I was able to see what I could do. I was able to see the difficulties he was facing. And it broke my heart that I was judging him. I want to thank Mr. Mushtak for that class and the activity and apologise to Ben. This activity has opened my eyes. And I urge my colleagues not to judge others and rather try to put themselves in their shoes."

Another powerful way to build relationships is through gratitude. Showing gratitude develops both those who receive it and those who deliver it. It also creates and touches others by providing a positive example. One memorable and impactful way to show gratitude is the "Gratitude Visit" described by Martin Seligman, the bestselling author and one of the leading researchers in positive psychology. Seligman used this technique in a positive psychology study in 2005, where the exercise resulted in a measurable positive psychological impact on those involved. To perform the exercise, you need to identify a person who had a positive impact on you and write them a thank you letter. The letter is ideally no more than one page long, written using very specific language showing why you are grateful and for what. Remember the particular thoughts and emotions associated with the impact you are thankful for, and record that. The letter can be structured in four parts as follows:

1. Start by being specific about what you are grateful for: For example, "Thank you for preparing the financial reports for me to use in my meeting, even before I ask you to do so."

2. Outline how this helped you succeed: For example, "This allowed us to have a very effective meeting and be able to make the right decisions promptly."

3. Recognise the effort and sacrifice: For example, "You did that despite your very busy schedule and having many deadlines to meet."

4. Praise the character strength: For example, "This speaks volumes to how a great team player you are. You always put the interest of the team ahead. We are truly blessed to have you around."

Once the letter is written, you will need to make an appointment to see the person to whom the letter is intended without telling them about the letter. Make it a surprise. When you meet the person, find the right moment and read the letter out loud to them. You may want to laminate or even frame the letter and present it as a gift that the recipient can hang on the wall or keep at their desks [2].

You may want to make gratitude a hallmark of your lifestyle and do these gratitude visits frequently to different individuals who have impacted you. To start a domino effect, suggest to the recipient of your letter that they can pay it forward and send a thank you note to a deserving individual.

Inspirational Leadership

Leadership is a human quality that is both important and difficult to define simultaneously. I define leadership as *the ability and willingness to exhibit initiative in the face of uncertainty and take responsibility for the results.* Leadership also entails having a deep sense of purpose and vision for a better future and readiness to serve others. It is important to remember that leadership is seldom about the position. Anyone with a purpose and vision for doing things better, to serve others and improve their life, and who takes the initiative to bring positive change while taking responsibility for their action can be described as a leader. I see this definition of leadership as liberating as it implies that any one of us can practice leadership without waiting to be officially appointed.

For those who hold an official position of leadership, the expectations are clear. They need to serve, show the way, be ready to take responsibility and face the consequences of their actions and decisions. They must be prepared to take the blame for failure and share credit for success.

Influence and Change

Emotionally intelligent individuals can positively influence those around them and be agents of constructive change in their environments. One such individual is Jack Sim, the founder of WTO (World Toilet Organisation). At the age of 40 and after starting 16 successful businesses, Jack Sim had what he called a mid-life crisis when he began to question his own purpose. Realising that millions of people around the world do not have access to proper toilets, Jack decided to do something about it. "I was an academic failure as I had no degree. I also had no status and no authority," Jack said. "Starting on a shoestring budget and the hope to change the world, I had no choice but to attempt to enact change through influencing others to act," he added. Jack calls his framework of change and influence O.P. (Other People). The idea is straightforward: if you are clever enough and have a worthy cause, you can leverage unlimited resources to your cause; these include Other People's money, talent, authority, time, power and brand.

Realising that there were a number of Toilet Organisations around the world, Jack founded the World Toilet Organisation in Singapore in 2001. He managed to convince various toilet organisations that it is a good idea to have their HQ in Singapore. From the start, Jack used humour to break the taboo associated with toilets. This began with him playing on the WTO acronym, which belongs to the World Trade Organisation. He went on to get himself photographed while wrapped in toilet paper and carrying a plunger. With a combination of humour and perseverance, Jack attracted media, business leaders, politicians and even Hollywood and Bollywood superstars to the cause. As a result, he was able to help many communities around the world, especially in India and Africa. In 2010, the World Toilet Organisation established the SaniShop to market and sell toilets to communities that need them the most. The business model of the SaniShop is based on enabling communities to build their own toilets and improve sanitation and health in the process. Over 15,000 toilets were sold in Cambodia before the Ministry of Rural Development took over the project. The success achieved in India was tremendous, as communities took advantage of government subsidies and built more than 110 million toilets.

Seeing that female toilets in public places often have a long queue compared to male toilets, Jack lobbied the Singaporean authorities to change the building code, increasing the ratio of female toilets to male toilets from 1:1 to 5:3 in public areas with heavy usage, such as shopping malls, cinemas, convention halls and MRT stations. For every three male cubicles or urinals, there will be five cubicles for females.

Jack continues influencing people (Other People, O.P., as he calls them) to act. His latest O.P. leverage is the production of a full-length feature comedy film, *"Everybody's Business."* The story of this Lee Thean Jeen movie revolves around 50 Singaporeans getting food poisoning because of toilet hygiene issues. The fictional Minister of Toilets, together with hygiene officers of the Ministry of Toilets, go around trying to reach the bottom of the matter. Once again, Jack uses humour to break the taboo and deliver the message.

When Jack spoke to my students, his advice was straightforward: If you know your purpose and believe in making a difference, then think of the abundance in the world around you. If you align "Other People" with your goals, the cause will always be the winner.

The United Nations recognised Jack Sim's efforts, and World Toilet Day is currently celebrated on the 19th of November.

Jack Sim. Founder of World Toilet Organisation

Managing Conflicts

As more and more human activities involve working with people from different backgrounds, cultures and nationalities, conflict may be inevitable, ranging from argument, disagreement, and emotional tension to fighting or war. The conflict often starts with a misunderstanding or disagreement; if parties agree to disagree, there will be no conflict. In the book *Hostage at the Table* by George Kohlieser, the following sources for conflict are identified:

1. Differences in Goals
2. Differences in Interests
3. Differences in Values
4. Differences in Communication styles
5. Differences in Power and Status
6. Insecurity
7. Resistance to Change
8. Role Confusion
9. Search for Ego Identity
10. Personal Needs
11. Poor Communication

To effectively manage conflicts, a bond between the conflicting parties needs to be maintained at all times. Couples with different religions, racial or political orientations can keep the bond and manage any conflicts that they may have. The misunderstanding that causes disagreement and conflict can stem from misunderstanding of oneself and misunderstanding of others. If we do not know what we want or what others want, or if we do not know how we feel or how others feel, misunderstanding can happen, and it can lead to conflict [3]. By now, you may have guessed that self-awareness is the antidote to misunderstanding of self, and social awareness is the antidote for misunderstanding others.

Practically, you can use the approach below to resolve conflict as described in *Resolving Conflict Creatively* by Linda Lantieri [4]:

1. Calm down, tune into your feelings, and express them.
2. Show a willingness to work things out by talking over the issue rather than escalating it with more aggression.
3. Try to find equitable ways to resolve the dispute, working together to find a resolution that both sides can embrace.

Issues Clearance

A structured way to resolve conflicts is called "Issues Clearance." It is a powerful way of resolving conflicts by acknowledging the role of stories and emotions in their creation. This technique requires training, discipline and commitment. Both sides taking part in the issues clearance process should have prior training in the technique for the best results. That is why this technique works better for teams and organisations where the members are familiar with both the process and the language of this technique. The process goes like this:

1. The individual having issues, A, approaches the person with whom they have issues, B, and says, "I have something important to talk to you about. Is this a good time?" You can also use an equivalent variation such as "I have an issue that I wish to clear with you. Is this a good time?"
2. Once the time to discuss the issue is agreed upon, individual A then states the facts of the matter by saying, "The facts are........." This is done by sticking to facts and avoiding any judgements.
3. Individual A then says, "The story I told myself is ...." Here, the individual can narrate their judgement of the matter and can use expressions like, "in my opinion....," "my judgement was...."
4. Then, individual A acknowledges their emotions by saying, "I feel ...." followed by describing the emotions associated with the issues being expressed. These may include sad, lonely, disrespected, afraid, confused, etc.
5. Individual A owns their role in the issues by saying, "My role in this is...." This critical stage gets the person to reflect on their role in creating or sustaining the situation.

6. Individual A states explicitly what they want by saying, "And I specifically want......."
7. Now, individual B reflects back by repeating the whole thing they have just heard: facts, story, the emotions associated, the role, and the wants. This is done without interpretation and with the spirit of trying to understand. The reflection is followed by a question by the reflector: "Is this accurate?" This reflection stage should be repeated until individual A is satisfied with its accuracy. This is very necessary so that individual A feels being listened to.
8. After completing the reflection, individual B asks, "Is there more?" This is asked in a genuine and curious manner.

Going through this process enables both parties to empathise with each other and examine their emotions and their role in creating and prolonging the conflict. This can promote mutual understanding and conflict resolution.

The following is a real example of using the Issues Clearance method; Tania (not her real name) was selected by the CEO of the organisation to be part of a strategic transformation team. Before launching the project, another team member called for a meeting for the team with the CEO to discuss the project scope and success measures. The other two team members and the CEO responded to the meeting invitation by accepting it. Tania was silent and had yet to respond to the meeting invitation. The other two members felt that Tania might not be a suitable team member and wanted to discuss this with the CEO. On the morning when the meeting was supposed to take place, the project leader asked to meet the CEO together with team members, apart from Tania, who came to the meeting even though she did not send a response to the meeting organiser. The team wanted to share with the CEO some concerns related to Tania's work style.

When Tania was asked to excuse herself while the rest of the team had a pre-meeting discussion with the CEO, she was unhappy as she left the room. The CEO promised the team members that he would make sure that Tania would be more sensitive and responsive to the team's needs, including responding to meeting invitations. After the meeting, Tania went to see the CEO to record that she was unhappy with how she was treated. The CEO suggested that Tania clears the issues with the team. The process went like this:

"Today, I went to the project meeting that you called for, and I was asked to leave the room," Tania started by stating the facts of the matter.

"The story I told myself was that the other team members did not want me to be in the team. In my opinion, the other team members are close friends, and they prefer to work without me," she continued by stating the story she told herself. "This made me feel rejected, sad and threatened," Tania added, acknowledging her emotions. "My role in creating this situation is that I did not communicate with the team members, and I did not respond to the meeting invite. I also assumed that asking me to excuse myself from the meeting is a threat to me," Tania continued as she acknowledged her role in the issue she was clearing. Finally, she stated that what she wanted was: "To be respected and appreciated."

The team leader reflected back to Tania what she had just narrated by saying, "I hear you say that you were asked to leave the meeting this morning. The story you told yourself is that the other team members did not want you to be in the team, and that made you feel sad, threatened and rejected. You acknowledged your role in creating the situation by the lack of communication on your part and by assuming that having the morning discussion without you was a threat. What you want for yourself is to be respected and appreciated. Is that accurate?" "Yes," Tania replied. The team leader followed by saying, "Is there more?" to which she replied, "No."

The team leader was able to reflect to Tania what she said because he listened carefully and kept an open mind. I witnessed situations where the reflection was repeated more than five times before it was accepted by the person clearing the issue as an accurate representation.

It is helpful to say here that the purpose of this process is not to get each party what they want but instead to get them to hear each other and put the conflict on the resolution path. This issue clearance process works well when both parties are willing to play by the rules of the method and are trained in using the technique.

For this specific example, the conflict was eventually resolved, and everyone on the team ended up appreciating the unique skills each team member brought to the table.

Teamwork and Collaboration

Teamwork is a necessary collaborative skill; it is difficult to imagine success without it. The challenges presented by today's complex environment can only be addressed by highly effective teams of people from different walks of life. Although teamwork is one of the highly sought-after skills, employers around the world are complaining that academic programmes are unable to equip graduates with the necessary skills to work well in teams. This section attempts to provide a simple and straightforward methodology to develop skills and techniques that can go a long way in ensuring sustainable team success.

Team Evolution

Teamwork is a complex human interaction that requires specific skills that can be learned and developed over time. This starts with understanding the various stages a group of people who are working together as a team usually go through. The Tuckman Model is one of the best models that describes how a team evolves and can provide helpful insight into human interaction in a team. The model has four stages presented on two axes: knowledge and enthusiasm, as shown below.

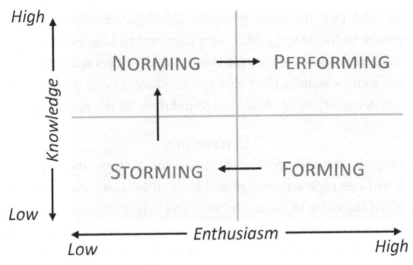

Tuckman Model for team evolution

Forming

Forming is the first stage of team evolution. The team members are usually selected because of their capabilities and skills related to the project. During this stage, the enthusiasm among the team members is typically high, but the knowledge of the tasks assigned to them and their teammates, as well as the team dynamics, is low.

Storming

As time passes and tasks accumulate, enthusiasm wears off, but knowledge may not necessarily grow. The combination of low enthusiasm and low knowledge leads to stress and conflict, and different team members respond differently; some will be disappointed and confused, whereas some will just withdraw. The storming stage is difficult, but it is necessary to progress towards the remaining team evolution stages. The key is to be able to recognise the symptoms of the storming stage when it happens and go through it swiftly.

Norming

The norming stage is where leadership potential shines. Typically, what happens is that some (at least one) of the team members take charge and pull the team members towards achieving the team's objectives. In this stage, enthusiasm may still be low, but knowledge and respect are definitely on the rise. Team members will start to taste success as they achieve their objectives and meet tasks deadlines. This stage is necessary to lay down the foundation for the next stage.

Performing

Building on the momentum of the norming stage, the performing stage features high knowledge and high enthusiasm. Arriving at this stage is a hallmark of successful teamwork. In this stage, respect and appreciation for team members' individual qualities are prevalent. Team members also have an accurate self-assessment of their own strengths and capabilities.

Team Building Exercises

After selecting the team members, we can accelerate and boost the team performance through various team-building exercises. These are activities that the team members can do together. Usually, team members will do some fun exercises as a group. These can include solving some interesting mental or physical challenges or even cooking. Through these exercises, team members get to appreciate each other and the diversity that they bring to the team. Team building can be done with newly formed or pre-existing teams that are given new tasks or wish to rekindle the team spirit.

It is also helpful for teams to agree on the rules of their interactions and engagements, write down these rules, and even display them as a reminder where the group often meets. In his book *Aspirations of Greatness*, Jim Warner gives an excellent example of such rules represented by the following 13 principles [5].

1. I will respect the confidentiality
2. I will be present in the moment
3. I will stay around when times get tough
4. I will be on time and stay until the end
5. I will speak my truth
6. I will ask for what I want
7. I will take care of myself
8. I will listen with curiosity and openness
9. I will own my judgements
10. I will own my feelings
11. I will not blame, shame or fix others
12. I will ask permission before offering feedback
13. I forgive myself and others for mistakes

The above 13 principles are beneficial to create a safe environment to tackle complex and challenging issues and progress the team when things are tough towards the performing stage.

Relationships as Social Capital

Back in the 1960s, a Ph.D. student at Harvard spoke to 282 men in the same town in the United States and asked each of them how they had got their job. The surprising results were that over 80% of those surveyed said they found their jobs through acquaintances or "friends of a friend." The paper where this research was published, *"The Strength of Weak Ties,"* [6] became one of the most cited papers in sociology. Said simply, who you know matters. The value of your relationships can be described as your "Social Capital."

Sixty years later, more current research shows that developing social capital is becoming even more critical in this age of the Fourth Industrial Revolution. Not only does it help people build better careers and deliver superior job performance, but it also gives access to more and better information and facilitates trust. In order to achieve genuine, sustainable and balanced success in life, we need to preserve, cultivate and manage five types of capital: human capital, social capital, emotional capital, natural capital and economic capital. This is true at individual, organisational and even national levels.

Human capital refers to the experience, skills, training, knowledge and know-how that we have acquired through our academic and professional credentials. Social capital is the value of the relationships and networks that we are part of. Emotional capital refers to our levels of emotional intelligence and our abilities to remain emotionally anchored and motivate ourselves and others. Natural capital, on the other hand, refers to nature and the environment of our planet. Acquired and appropriately used, social capital can positively leverage and enhance all the different types of capital.

Despite their importance, current education systems focus on the development of human capital with very little intentional emphasis on the development of other types of capital and the skills needed to build professional networks. This chapter explores pathways we can use to initiate and nurture social capital. We have to start by realising that social capital is not how many we are connected to on social media. It is who will return our phone call, email, or text when we need some help or support.

Scholars have shown that people do not benefit from networks passively. They need to mobilise these networks to get the benefit from them. To build successful professional networks, the following advice can be helpful:

1. Map your existing network by identifying the people you already know and the networks these people belong to. These can be your family members, friends or even teachers and lecturers if you are a student. Make sure that you keep a good relationship with those in your network and be helpful to them by supporting them in achieving their professional goals.

2. Identify the networks you would like to be part of and use your current contacts and the "friends of friends" to introduce you. Some networks are more difficult to penetrate than others, but an introduction is always helpful. Remember that the most resourceful network that you can tap into could be the Alumni network of your institution or school.

3. Build a professional online presence. LinkedIn is an excellent platform for this. Use a professional profile picture and describe your skills, experiences and career goals in a clear manner.

4. If you are still a student, join suitable student societies and chapters representing the professional body that you are interested in. Be an active member of these societies through participation in organising events and running for leadership positions.

5. Volunteer with a charity that resonates with your core values and the impact you wish to have on the world. Volunteering is great for meeting highly motivated, supportive, like-minded individuals.

6. Help the network become stronger by introducing people you know to each other if you feel that it is beneficial to both parties to be introduced. Be generous with your support to other members of the network, support their events and send them personalised messages to celebrate their success.

The above list is one aspect of the structured approach I encourage my students to use when building and growing their professional networks and social capital.

Whether we realise it or not, we are all related. The intentional development of supportive professional networks is a key element of creating value in the web of relationships that connects all. Through that, we will be able to generate and enhance social capital for ourselves, our businesses and the nation.

RELATIONSHIP MANAGEMENT

Our happiness is ultimately measured by

THE QUALITY of the relationships we have with our loved ones and those around us.

Have a **MISSION PARTNER** so that you support each others as you go about actualising your Mission.

Perform a GRATITUDE VISIT

Write a Thank You Letter that has these 3 parts

● Identify the Benefit
● Recognise the Effort
● Praise the Strength

Visit the intended person
Read the letter out loud to her/him

Have a TEAM CHARTER

List the rules of engagement that govern how the team members should communicate and interact with each other. The team charter should be agreed upon by the team members and preferably displayed for the members to be able to refer to easily.

Use "ISSUE CLEARANCE" to resolve conflict

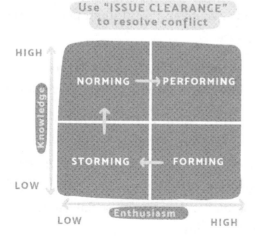

Work with others
IN TEAMS

and be aware of the team development stages.

9

Telling the Story

"A man's character may be learned from the adjectives which he habitually uses in conversation."

Mark Twain

In a fascinating social experiment known as "Significant Objects," writers Rob Walker and Joshua Glenn explored the profound appeal of storytelling within the human psyche. They purchased seemingly ordinary thrift shop items for an average of USD1.25 each and then enlisted over 200 professional writers to craft short stories inspired by these mundane objects. The items were then posted on eBay for auction accompanied by the short stories rather than the usual item description. [1]

The results of the experiment were nothing short of extraordinary. Some of these thrift shop finds were ultimately sold for nearly USD8,000, a staggering 6,300% Return on Investment. This suggests that the stories had a profound impact on the perceived value of the objects.

What is it about storytelling that can so effectively shape our perception of the world around us? Exposure to well-structured and delivered stories triggers the release of neurotransmitters, such as cortisol, dopamine, oxytocin and endorphin, in the brain resulting in feelings of trust, engagement and even fear and anxiety. This gives stories the potential to tap into our "affective forecasting" abilities. This is our ability to predict how we will feel in a given situation. Listening to well-told stories, we project ourselves into the narrative and imagine ourselves experiencing the events first-hand. This, in turn, can lead us to assign a greater value to the object that is the focus of the story.

The "Significant Objects" experiment provides a powerful illustration of the power of storytelling. It suggests that we can use stories to shape the way others perceive us, our products and our ideas. If we can effectively tap into the emotional core of our audience, we can create a sense of connection and understanding that can lead to greater persuasion and influence.

I hope that by now, we have established the importance of the stories we tell in our heads in shaping our lives and the lives of those around us. Our ability to communicate, educate, motivate and lead change depends on our ability to encourage others to change their stories and build environments in which better stories thrive. One of the best ways to communicate and inspire is through telling great stories. In this chapter, we will explore communication strategies that we can use to tell exceptional stories and communicate effectively.

Communication Strategies

Every day, from the moment we wake up to the moment we go to sleep, we are continuously communicating. Even if we do not notice, the advertisements on billboards as we go to work or school and the websites that we visit are always trying to communicate their messages to us. Companies want us to buy their products, and they try to articulate why we need them and how they are superior to others. We communicate with our team members, friends, parents, and children, seeking their cooperation and understanding. In one way or another, communication aims to convey messages and achieve a behavioural change in the targeted audience. Salespeople want to communicate how superior their products are (message) and want their customers to buy those products (behaviour), teachers want to share knowledge (message) and want their students to learn (behaviour) and politicians wish to communicate their political views and policies (message) and want the citizens to vote for them (behaviour). In this context, it is fair to say that successful communication is when the right message is communicated to the right audience, and it stays in their mind to create the desired behaviour. To be consistent with the message of this book, we can also say that often the objective of communication is to redirect the stories the members of the audience tell in their minds, and what better way to change someone's story than with another story?

In his book, *TED Talks: The Official TED Guide to Public Speaking*, Chris Anderson gave two examples of how to tell and how not to tell a story. The two examples describe the same situation. Here is how the story should be told. "Once, when I was eight years old, my father took me fishing. We were in a tiny boat, five miles from shore, when a massive storm blew in. Dad put a life jacket on me and whispered in my ear, "Do you trust me, son?" I nodded. He threw me overboard. I kid you not. Just tossed me over! I hit the water and bobbed up to the surface, gasping for breath. It was shockingly cold. The waves were terrifying. Monstrous. Then, Dad dived in after me. We watched in horror as our little boat flipped and sank. But he was holding me the whole time, telling me it was going to be okay. Fifteen minutes later, the Coast Guard helicopter arrived. It turned out that Dad knew the boat was damaged and was going to sink, and he had called them with our exact location. He guessed it was better to chuck me in the open sea than risk getting trapped when the boat flipped. And that is how I learned the true meaning of the word trust."

Here's how not to tell the same story. "I learned trust from my father when I was eight years old, and we got caught in a storm while out fishing for mackerel. We failed to catch a single one before the storm hit. Dad knew the boat was going to sink because it was one of those Saturn brand inflatable boats, which are usually pretty strong, but this one had been punctured once, and Dad thought it might happen again. In any case, the storm was too big for an inflatable boat, and it was already leaking. So he called the Coast Guard rescue service, who, back then, were available 24/7, unlike today. He told them our location, and then, to avoid the risk of getting trapped underwater, he put a life jacket on me and threw me overboard before jumping in himself. We then waited for the Coast Guard to come and, sure enough, 15 minutes later, the helicopter showed up—I think it was a Sikorsky MH-60 Jayhawk—and we were fine."

Chris Anderson goes on saying "The first story has a character you care about and intense drama that builds to incredulity before being beautifully resolved. The second version is a mess. The drama is killed by revealing the father's intent too early, there's no attempt to share the actual experience of the kid, and there are too many details included that are irrelevant to most of the audience, while other germane details like the giant waves are ignored. Worst of all, the key line that anchors the story, "Do you trust me, son?" is lost. If you're going to tell a story, make sure you know why you're telling it, and try to edit out all the details that are not needed to make your point while still leaving enough in for people to vividly imagine what happened." [2]

Communication can be verbal or non-verbal. In the book titled *The Tipping Point*, Malcolm Gladwell explored a number of ideas that "stuck" and became phenomena that were talked about, shared, and eventually changed history [3]. Inspired by Gladwell's book, Chip and Dan Heath wrote their book *Made to Stick* and identified the features that an idea, a story or a communicated message can aspire to have in order for it to stick and result in a change of behaviour of the receiver. *Made to Stick* utilises a framework that uses the acronym SUCCES, which stands for Simple, Unexpected, Concrete, Credible, Emotional and Stories [3]. I added another S, "Show, not only tell." The message or story need not have all the seven elements of the SUCCESS framework, but having three or more of these elements improves its chances of being remembered and having an impact. I shall describe each part of the SUCCESS framework in the sections below.

Simple

This is one of the most critical components of the SUCCESS framework, and we should always strive to incorporate it into our storytelling and communication strategies. People will always remember simple stories and messages better than complex ones. The interesting thing is that, often, simple is more difficult to achieve than complex. To simplify anything, one must be very well-versed in all of its aspects. Apple products, for example, are known to be simple and easy to use; this simplicity is the outcome of the labour of many designers and engineers who worked tirelessly to fully comprehend how the products are to be used and designed them for a memorable user experience. In short, simple is not easy. One of Picasso's paintings, The Bull, illustrates this concept well. Picasso drew 11 paintings of a bull, starting with a life-like drawing of the bull and progressively removing parts of it in a quest to reach the essence of the bull. The eleventh painting uses only a few lines to represent the bull. It is simple, but Picasso reached this simplicity through his mastery of the complex.

If you have an idea, a message or a concept that you wish to communicate, you will need first to really comprehend its essence. This essence can be the basis of your communication strategy. You will need to be able to explain your concept with as few words as possible, stripping any part that is not core to the message. Simple messages are compact and profound while conveying the core essence of what needs to be communicated. Just like in the story narrated above by Chris Anderson, several details were intentionally removed while maintaining the essence, which is learning about trust.

Picasso's "The Bull". (Source: takeovertime.co)

Using metaphors is another way of simplifying communication. The word metaphor is from the Greek word "metaphora", which means to transfer. So, a metaphor is a mental shortcut in which we can use a familiar concept to communicate a less familiar one by transferring our understanding of the existing concept to the new one. When DNA was introduced as evidence in criminal justice, lawyers and judges struggled with understanding and accepting it. One way to communicate how DNA can help in delivering justice was the metaphor introducing DNA as the new fingerprint.

Unexpected

"Bill Gates just released mosquitoes into the audience at TED and said, 'Not only poor people should experience this.'" This was a tweet by Dave Morin, who witnessed Bill Gates releasing mosquitoes into the hall during his TED talk about malaria. The mosquitoes did not carry malaria. Nonetheless, releasing them to the audience is probably the last thing you would expect during a talk about malaria. This act has, for sure, grabbed the attention of many, went viral on social media and was very memorable [5].

We have explored the role the old brain plays in responding to what is perceived as a threat. This part of the brain is wired to make us react quickly to situations that are out of the ordinary, and it is responsible for the fight-or-flight reaction. That is why shocking, surprising, and unexpected events or information seize our attention more than expected ones. If you go for a lecture on your first day at university and your Thermodynamics lecturer arrives in a blue suit and a black tie, this will not be remarkable. However, if he instead arrives in a clown outfit, I bet you will always remember this lecture, even after a long time. You may even remember the second law of thermodynamics better as a result. Always look for an unexpected hook or angle to pitch or deliver your message. The unexpectedness can be achieved through how the message is crafted, the medium used to deliver it or who delivers it.

Blendtec is a company that makes blenders, and to advertise how strong their blenders are, they made a series of videos showing them in action. They did not demonstrate their blenders mixing fruits and vegetables; instead, they did something highly unexpected. They filmed their blenders mixing everything from golf balls to iPhones. These videos are in a series of videos called *Will it blend?* I watched the "blending" of an iPhone 5S and 4 iPhone 5Cs (the full-colour range), and the blender turned them into dust. This video has over 2 million views on YouTube. *Will it Blend?* Videos are also available at *https://blendtec.com/pages/will-it-blend*. This sure had an impact on me, as I am planning to buy one of these blenders.

When my school wanted to put a newspaper advertisement to promote engineering as a career option, we looked for an unexpected angle to pitch that. While a typical advertisement promoting engineering may talk about the role of engineers in building different technological gadgets, we used the fact that 33% of CEOs of the world's top 500 companies have an engineering degree as the ad's main point. According to The Business Insider, only 11% of these CEOs have a first degree in business administration. Many people find this to be unexpected and rather amazing. When the advertisement appeared in a local paper, it had a very good impact on our intended audience, and many parents and students had a reinforced view that engineering is a flexible and exciting career pathway.

Credible

For the message to be effectively communicated and achieve its intended impact, it needs to be credible. This means that the new brain needs to believe it. If Blendtec wants to prove that their blenders are strong, running an advertisement of them blending iPhones is not only remarkably unexpected but also credible. There are several ways to lend credibility to a given message. In our engineering advertisement mentioned earlier, we needed to reference The Business Insider newspaper as the party that performed the research, which showed that 33% of the CEOs of the world's top 500 companies are engineers. This was an independent study that the public has access to and can check out for themselves. Endorsements by users or professionals can lend credibility to some products. Toothpaste companies, for example, enlist the help of dentists to endorse their products.

Barry Marshal is an Australian scientist who had a revolutionary idea. While the medical community believed that stomach ulcers are caused by stress and a diet of spicy food with basically no cure, Dr. Marshal had a different idea. He thought the ulcer was caused by bacteria and was treatable by antibiotics. The prevailing wisdom was that the stomach was too acidic for any bacteria to live in it. Faced with a community that did not believe him, he did the ultimate: he infected himself with the bacteria, resulting in an ulcer in his stomach. After the disease was officially diagnosed, Dr. Marshal successfully treated his ulcer with antibiotics. This discovery had a significant impact on hundreds of thousands of people who have stomach ulcers and eventually earned Barry Marshal the Nobel Prize [6].

Concrete

It is easier to comprehend concrete concepts as compared to abstract ones. This is particularly true when dealing with technological terminology. For example, if you are contemplating buying a smartphone, you will know that the 32GB option will have double the capacity of the 16GB. But do you really know how much is 16GB? Imagine communicating the capacity of the phone by how many photos or songs it can store or how many hours of video it can accommodate. Everyone can relate to the photos, songs, and videos because they represent concrete concepts.

Successful marketing campaigns and communication strategies need to differentiate their claims from those of the competitors in a concrete manner in order for them to be effective. So, suppose the product or service you are promoting is better, bigger, cheaper, faster or more effective than the competition; in that case, your message needs to deliver this clearly and understandably. For example, if you want people to donate to charity and your message is intended to say that even a little bit can help vaccinate children in countries where vaccines are not available, the message can be "For the price of a cup of coffee, we can vaccinate one child against polio." Comparing the cost of the polio vaccine to the price of something ubiquitous in our everyday life, such as coffee, makes the impact of a donation very clear and can lead to more people willing to donate. If the message is delivered through a visual medium, a picture of a cup of coffee next to a healthy, vaccinated child can also be very impactful.

Emotional

Earlier in the book, we mentioned that emotions are processed in the middle brain. The relationship between emotions and decision-making was also examined. With this in mind, it is clear that messages with a healthy dose of emotions will have a better chance of being remembered and changing one's behaviour. Research has shown that when we receive a message, we are most likely to remember and respond if this message was delivered emotionally. That is why organisations fighting a particular disease among children, for example, put pictures of children on their marketing materials when they ask you for donations.

The trick is, when you develop a communication strategy to sell a product, service or idea, you need to communicate how the audience will feel when they buy your product, use your service or adopt your idea. So if the product is a phone, do not only mention the features. Instead, focus also on what the user will do with the phone. This would include pictures showing the users connecting with their loved ones, being successful at work (productivity apps), reaching their destinations safely (GPS app) and having fun with friends (entertainment apps).

Stories

We all enjoy good stories. We liked them when we were kids, and we continue to like them as adults. A good story represents a better way to remember and is always nice to share. If you are running a tutoring centre, a success story about an average-performing student who managed to join an engineering course after taking math and physics classes at your centre is an excellent way to say that you provide quality service. The message can be even more credible if the student tells it.

When telling a story or delivering a presentation, you need to pay special attention to how you start and end your presentation or your story. Our minds seem to pay special attention to the beginnings and ends of stories and presentations. This is probably the reason why most of the stories that our parents told us as children began with "Once upon a time...." and ended with "....... and they lived happily ever after." If you try to recall the last movie you watched, there is a good chance that you remember its beginning and end in more detail than the rest of the movie. Hollywood understands that, and directors pay special attention to making the beginnings and endings of their movies more sensational.

Next time you deliver a presentation promoting an idea, a product or a service, you may want to begin your "show" by outlining the pain your audience is experiencing (and hopefully how your product, service or idea can help alleviate it). You can use combinations of simple, unexpected, credible, concrete and/or emotional facts, data, and pictures to drive home the message. This beginning must be short and direct to keep those listening to you engaged and stays in their minds. The body of your presentation can discuss different features, aspects and capabilities of your idea, product or service. In concluding your presentation, you may again use a combination of simple, unexpected, credible, concrete and/or emotional messages outlining how your audience would feel after adopting your idea, product or service. This way, you will ensure that your core messages are fresh and present when your customers make their decisions.

Show, not only tell

Seeing is believing, and showing is a powerful tool to put the audience of a communicated message in a receptive frame of mind. Whenever possible, it is helpful to get the intended users to try the product, service, or idea being promoted. Producers give free samples of their products to allow consumers to experience them. Subscription-based services such as magazines or satellite channels can provide free subscriptions for a period to enable the customers to experience the service. Nowadays, most apps have free versions, allowing users to try the app before committing to purchase the full version. The Ikea and Apple Stores are perfect examples of this concept, where customers are encouraged to use and play around with the products.

Armed with the above SUCCESS framework, you will be able to structure your communication strategies to achieve your desired objectives. The framework will definitely be helpful if you are giving a presentation, designing a poster or billboard advertisement, directing a documentary or producing a product catalogue.

COMMUNICATE WITH A STORY

Communication will stick and inspire change if it uses the

SUCCESS Framework*

 Simple

 Unexpected

 Credible

 Concrete

 Emotional

 told with a **S**tory

 Show, not only tell

* Made to Stick by
Dan & Chip Heath

(This page is intentionally left blank)

10

Shoot the Boss:
Leadership and Emotional Intelligence

"If any blame or fault attaches to the attempt, it is mine alone."
General Dwight Eisenhower,
a speech to be delivered in case the Normandy invasion failed

Leaders and organisations that are aware and socially and relationally connected are not only more liked, but they are more likely to achieve their business objectives. This makes a strong business case for developing emotionally intelligent leadership. In this chapter, we will explore examples of leadership where individuals and organisations have transformed the individual and organisational narrative to achieve their goals.

A Crisis of Leadership

Do you think that the world suffers from a crisis of leadership? 86% of the 1,767 experts who responded to a 2015 World Economic Forum Survey on the Global Agenda think so. Should we be surprised by this? While the headline survey result may be shocking, the apparent failure of leadership to deal with the existential challenges faced in today's world might be behind this perception. Challenges that start with climate change and do not end with global inequality, geopolitical instability, economic and health crises are making the world more Volatile, Uncertain, Complex, and Ambiguous (VUCA). These are challenging issues for leaders at every level.

Interestingly, though, this apparent lack of faith in leaders is happening just as a global recognition of the importance of leadership is emerging. Schools and universities are making leadership a staple part of their curriculum and educational outcomes, organisations are investing more than ever in leadership development, and the leadership section at the bookstores is growing daily. What is going on?

The crisis of leadership seems to emanate, at least in part, from the contradictions between what markets currently reward leaders for and what the world needs. Let us examine three of the dimensions where these contradictions are more profound:

1. Timescale: While many of the challenges we face require very long-term thinking, short-termism is rampant. Leaders can be under pressure to deliver quick results or pay a hefty price.

2. Sphere of focus: Despite all the rhetoric, many organisations measure results with an internal focus on their individual success rather than the success of the entire ecosystem. This influences the decisions leaders make.

3. Competition versus collaboration: While no single individual, organisation, or even country will ever be able to address the biggest challenges of our time, such as climate change or inequality alone, we still see nationalism, populism, price wars, and even outright war happening around us. Leaders often find it challenging to balance the fine line between competing and the need to work together for the common good.

We need a new breed of leaders who can deliver immediate results without sacrificing the long-term viability of their organisations, sectors, and even the world. These leaders need to possess an ecosystem mindset and be capable of finding commonalities and building consensus with competing and disagreeing parties while driving the agendas and interests of their institutions and communities.

These leaders will need to master several attributes, values, and skills, including a deep sense of purpose, being self-aware, and having the effectiveness and soft skills to be able to deliver a positive impact to their constituencies and the wider world. We call these purpose-driven leaders. Having a clear sense of purpose at the individual and organisational levels can go a long way in empowering leaders to both do well and do good.

Leadership and Accountability

The invasion of Normandy by the Allied forces on the 6th of June 1944 was a pivotal moment in the history of World War II. It opened the door to the liberation of Europe and the final defeat of Nazi Germany. General Dwight Eisenhower was the commander of the operation, and while he did all that he could to plan the campaign, he had his doubts. The enemy that he was facing was well-trained, well-entrenched and battle toughened. The stakes could not have been higher. General Eisenhower knew that he was sending tens of thousands of Allied soldiers to their deaths and their sacrifices better not be in vain. We now know the result of the Normandy invasion and the impact it had on the direction of the war. General Eisenhower gave a speech after the success of the invasion, encouraging his men and acknowledging the sacrifices they made. Most interestingly, though, he wrote another speech on the 5th of June, one day before sending the troops on their way. He prepared that speech to be delivered in case of failure of the invasion. The speech, which Eisenhower did not have to deliver, went like this: "Our landings in the Cherbourg-Havre area have failed to gain a satisfactory foothold, and I have withdrawn the troops. My decision to attack at this time and place was based upon the best information available. The troops, the Air and the Navy did all that bravery and devotion to duty could do. If any blame or fault attaches to the attempt it is mine alone."

This short speech and the circumstances in which it was written are very instructive. They teach us a few lessons about what leadership is all about. General Eisenhower had doubts, and the possibility of failure was real and potentially disastrous, but despite those doubts, he took calculated risks and made his decision. This is leadership. He also set his mind to take the full blame for failure, should it happen. This is accountability. Leadership is the ability to provide direction and vision in the face of uncertainty. It is about making the best decisions based on the available data, sharing the credit for success with others and accepting responsibility for failure.

Shooting the Boss

The lesson we learn from the example set by Eisenhower is that accountability is a crucial component of leadership. While, fortunately, not all the decisions we make are of the weight of the Normandy landing, setting our internal story to accept responsibility for failure can be a hugely empowering step for the leaders and those around them.

In 2013, our school was preparing for a major accreditation exercise. To successfully complete this exercise, academic staff needed to participate in very tedious planning and documentation processes. The time commitment to perform the preparation and documentation was not trivial and academics around the world dread it and view it as a necessary evil. We thought of a way to transform the staff experience and achieve genuine buy-in, so we came up with a process that we called "Shoot the Boss." It involved providing the staff with workshops as well as training and support sessions over six months to get them ready for the accreditation exercise. This included a mock accreditation exercise performed by experienced auditors. Staff were informed that the management had full confidence in them. While the success of the accreditation exercise depends on them, the management is taking full responsibility for any failure. The process concluded at a paintball court, where the entire staff force attended, and each one was asked three questions to assess their level of preparation and readiness. I informed the members of staff that if any of them failed to answer at least 2 out of the 3 questions correctly, that person is required to shoot me with the paintball marker as this is a sign that I have failed to give them the proper preparation or convince them of the importance of the accreditation exercise. I was the dean then and wanted to show my colleagues I took full responsibility for the accreditation results. Generally, the team did very well, and one lecturer was emotional when she missed the correct answers for some questions as she thought she answered correctly and did not want to shoot me.

After the "Shoot the Boss" session, we played a couple of paintball games and went for a great lunch together. Two months later, we had the actual accreditation visit and I was deeply touched to receive the accreditation report. Not only was it positive with all our programmes being accredited, but the accreditation committee recognised "highly motivated staff and students" as one of the strengths of the school. Now, whenever alignment is needed, people at the university say we need to "Shoot the Boss." I learned from this session that when the leaders are willing to serve, communicate the vision clearly and show full accountability, people are more than willing to support and pull together and even the most tedious task can become enjoyable.

Delivering Happiness

"You are now connected to Lili from Zappos.com." This is how my online chat session with Zappos started. I got to know about Zappos, a company that sells shoes and other clothing items online, from a book written by the company's CEO, the late Tony Hsieh. The book is titled *Delivering Happiness* and talks about how Zappos revolutionised the sales of shoes online through legendary customer service. The company achieved phenomenal growth and was later sold to Amazon for 1.2 billion US Dollars. Its extraordinary success emanated from the fact that the company used a fascinating narrative: "We are not in the shoe business; we are in the business of delivering happiness." Staff are told to do whatever it takes to make the customers happy. To ensure that only those who believe in the company's mission to deliver happiness are employed, Zappos has a strange practice. One week into the four-week immersive training programme the new hires are put through, the company makes them "The Offer." If you leave now, you will be paid for the time spent plus 2,000 US Dollars. [1] This obsession with customer service and focus on selecting employees who will do anything to deliver that is genuinely remarkable.

Shoot the Boss

I contacted Zappos to buy a present for my son. It turned out that they do not deliver outside the United States. Nonetheless, my chat with Lili lasted 70 minutes. I wanted to ask her more about the company, and she was happy to chat. Below are some segments from the chat that I had with Lili.

Me: I would like to buy a present for my son. He is 14 years old and likes photography and soccer. What is trending and would be suitable for him?

Lili: Mushtak, we do not have anything for photography, but I can recommend some soccer cleats.

Me: Great!

Lili: What size does he wear?

Me: 7 or 8, depending on the design.

Lili: OK, great. Here are the options we have.

Lili: http://www.zappos.com/soccer-cleats#!/

Me: Nice!

Me: By the way, do you deliver worldwide? I am in Malaysia now.

Lili: Unfortunately, we do not currently offer international shipping. We ship to all US States and Territories. You are welcome to place an order using an international credit card, but the shipping address must be within the United States.

Me: :-(

Lili: I'm so sorry!

Me: I am very interested in Zappos after reading Tony Hsieh's book Delivering Happiness. Your customer service is legendary.

Lili: Thank you. We appreciate that so much!

Me: I read that your staff are offered money to quit the company in the first month, is that correct?

Lili: Yes, during the training process. If someone is willing to leave Zappos, the company will pay them. It's amazing!

Me: Amazing indeed! Were you offered that too?

Lili: Oh, yes, and I didn't take it. I have been here for almost five years and am very happy!

Me: What makes Zappos such a happy place to work?

Lili: I believe in the independence that the company gives us. We are all treated like family.

Me: How is the value of "delivering happiness" operationalised at Zappos? With the independence you are given, how does the company ensure that happiness is delivered?

Lili: We are given the tools to make customers happy.

Me: I heard some customers contact you to chat, and you entertain them. Is this something that the company encourages?

Lili: We do. We try to resolve their issues first, and then we can chat until they are satisfied.

Me: I will mention my conversation with you in my new book.

Lili: That's amazing, Mushtak. Please do!

Me: The idea of the book is very simple: we all tell stories in our minds that end up shaping who we are. Great leaders and great companies are able to make people change their stories to be more positive and inspirational. I believe that Zappos is a great story that all of you tell. And that is why I am very interested in the company.

Lili: Very true. Everyone has their own perception of their story here at Zappos. Don't get me wrong. Sometimes, we have issues. We have a ton of questions when things move around, but communication is key. Everyone works as a team to get it resolved. That is the true power of Zappos.

Me: Did you change the stories you tell yourself as a result of your work, Zappos?

Lili: When I first started, yes. It was unreal how things were not the way I thought they would be.

Me: How was that?

Lili: Well, at first, when you get hired, the trainers tell you that you literally can do whatever you need to make the customer happy. There was no restriction, but abuse was not acceptable. However, when I started work, I had doubts that the company meant we could do anything to make the customers happy. Boy, was I wrong! That is the best part of my job is to fix things. I had a customer tell me that I was a "YES" woman. Haha!

Me: That is really powerful. I am sure this was transformational for you.

Lili: Now, when I see new people, I love to speak to them because they all have the same thought process when I was hired.

Me: You are amazing, actually. What was the longest chat you had with a customer?

Lili: Thank you! It was about 5 hours, a customer needed some items for a wedding, and she was about three months pregnant. It was really fun. She still chats in from time to time and asks about me.

Me: What else can you tell me to include in my book?

Lili: Hmm, well, we love to have fun. We have a party after the holidays to celebrate hard work. We also have a bistro, and the company feeds us really yummy food. We do not have a dress code. We can wear whatever we want. Style is not an issue.

Me: It is 2:49 a.m. in Las Vegas now. Have a great morning, then.

Lili: It is very early, and I started my coffee.

Me: Stay awesome! I hope we can chat again in the future.

Lili: Likewise, I'm sure we will.

After finishing the chat with Lili, I thought to myself, what other company encourages its representatives to chat for more than an hour without the prospect of making a sale? I will look forward to the day that Zappos delivers worldwide, and I shall recommend them to anyone who wants to buy the products they sell.

Competing Against Cancer

In 1990, the authors of *Tribal Leadership* were performing research for their book in which they identified four stages of organisational culture [2]. These were:

1. Stage One: Members of a stage one organisation (tribe) are bitter, hostile and cynical. They feel detached from other tribe members, and individually, they tell themselves stories of the nature: "Life is unfair, and I have no chance at making it any better. My work is never appreciated, and life is hopeless." This is a dysfunctional stage, and very few organisations can remain there for long without disintegrating.

2. Stage Two: This is where 25% of the organisations are. Members of these tribes gave up on each other. They are indifferent and have a sense of uselessness. Members blame the management all the time, and while they are able to do their basic jobs, they are unable to innovate or exhibit initiative. They tell themselves stories of the sort: "We are incapable of doing great work."

3. Stage Three: This is where 49% of the workplaces are. Members of tribes at this stage are selfish and self-centred. They withhold information and knowledge from their colleagues and want to succeed without regard for the other tribe members. Individually, they tell themselves stories like "I'm great . . . and you're not."

4. Stage Four: Tribe members at this stage share a common vision. They work together collaboratively and focus their competitive

spirit against other competing tribes. They tell themselves stories like "We're great . . . and they're not."

Towards the tail end of their research process, the authors of *Tribal Leadership* interviewed the staff and management of Amgen, a pharmaceutical company, and asked them who their competitors were. If this company were to exhibit the Stage Four culture, the answer would've been "Genentech" or "Pfizer". To the authors' surprise, team after team within Amgen, when asked about who they compete against, they gave answers of the type: "We're in competition with cancer," or "Our competitor is an inflammatory disease." This led the authors to conclude that there exists a fifth tribal stage in which tribe members have a great sense of purpose that they draw the meaning of their existence from. Members tell themselves stories such as, "We are here to make a difference and have a positive impact on the world and make life great for everyone."

It is very interesting to see that the level of success and impact of an organisation is reflected in and affected by the language and narrative told within these organisations. This is a further indication that changing the language used in an organisation and creating an environment within which positive narratives take root are essential ingredients for achieving sustainable success.

When a Company Abolished the P-word

Robert Newman is the CEO of MiTeGen, a small company that manufactures and distributes products for crystallisation and crystallography. He registered for the *Success with Emotional Intelligence* course. He found the concept of abolishing the P-word to be "an excellent way to teach about re-framing and context, and how language matters more than we realise!"

"Earlier this year, we held a Kaizen Blitz event for four days at my company to improve many processes related to vendor management. I implemented the idea of banishing the P-word (replacing it with

"Opportunity" or "Challenge") and gave each Kaizen team member $10 in ones. If someone used the word "problem" or "can't", the one that caught the slip got $1 from them. It was a fun way to help change language and mindset. Nobody left with less than $5 as they all learned to re-frame before opening their mouths. Additionally, the practice has carried forward, and my teams are getting good at re-framing and rewording without using the P-word!" Robert added.

"I did have one interesting emotional resistance to deal with, though. One engineer assigned a very strong sense of personal value in the fact that he was a problem solver and he prided himself on solving difficult technical problems. So, for that person, the P-word already meant what challenge and opportunity mean to most, and "removing" the P-word felt initially like a solid personal loss. It was as if we were lowering his self-worth or value to the team by not using the P-word! In the end, and through a private discussion. I think he was able to understand how the P-word affected others negatively, which was different from how it actually inspired him.

"The manager or teacher cannot escape their responsibility of knowing each team member or student and verifying how this works or doesn't work for the individual," Robert concluded.

As an engineer myself, I do appreciate the sense of identity engineers draw from being "problem solvers." After prolonged discussions, the alternative many engineers accepted, so they could remove the P-word, is for them to see themselves as "solutions providers."

11

The Awesomeness Club

"Real education is the process of inspiring people to tell more empowering stories about themselves and the world we live in."

The students who took my *Success with Emotional Intelligence* course have numerous winnings to report. The course community decided to create a section on the course website that we called the "Awesomeness Club," and we agreed to report significant winnings that resulted from the course's teachings in that section. Years after launching the course, participants still report amazing stories on the Awesomeness Club and below are some of these stories as they are told by their heroes. I hope these stories bring together the entire human development framework and show us how ordinary people achieve their goals by following the simple exercises outlined in this book.

Conquering Self to Conquer a Mountain

Luis is a 28-year-old technician from Santiago, Chile. He registered for the course to become more effective and successful but said, "I found the course to give me more than that. It gave me an important foundation for both my professional and personal life. Topics like the brain rewiring, self-awareness, social awareness, self-management and communication for success are essential for everyone." He decided to replace the P-word with the word opportunity. He has been applying this technique in different areas of his life, particularly mountaineering, where one would encounter many challenges, including weather, high altitude and tiredness along the journey. He now climbs with a positive attitude because he has changed his point of view from looking at things as challenges to opportunities; he says that "nowadays, climbing difficult mountains is no longer a P-word but rather a big challenge and great opportunity to develop myself, because I changed my point of view from P-word to challenge and opportunity."

One of the examples of this emotional shift was when he was climbing San Ramon Mountain, which is 3,253 meters above sea level. They were 3 hours from the summit when he stopped and sat down, hungry, tired and thirsty; his friend asked him, "What's up mate?" he answered, "It's just that the summit looks too far." After walking the last day to reach the base camp, he thought it was fair to think of giving up with all the "P-words" up ahead. But he remembered the poster he was carrying on the climb, "Don't say the P-word, just live your dreams", and at that precise moment, there was an emotional shift. He found renewed strength and took that as an opportunity to challenge himself to reach the summit. He said to himself, "Hey Luis, this is a great opportunity to challenge yourself. Go on and fight for it." Without that mental and emotional shift, we would not be reading his story or enjoying the wonderful picture of the San Ramon Mountain summit he has shared.

Success with Emotional Intelligence has been an excellent change for Luis. He went on to share, "I am more effective now, and I make better decisions both in my professional and personal life. Making the shift required a great will, and my family has noticed the change in me, telling me that I have a better disposition towards them, which is really important for me to hear."

Luis on the top of San Ramon Mountain with the Message "Don't Say the P-Word- Just Live Your Dreams"

When Stammering Becomes a Friend

Michael, a course participant from India, found public speaking challenging due to his stammer. Below is an account of how, with the help of the activities in the course, he managed to overcome his public speaking challenge.

Michael was given an opportunity to deliver a speech, but he seriously considered declining because of his stammer. However, he finally decided this was an opportunity to face his fears and shift his focus towards what was more positive: the people who wanted to listen to what he had to say. He carefully crafted his speech and visualised himself speaking confidently to his audience, articulating each word slowly but clearly. He also decided to rename that stammer from a P-word to a friend who visits him when he is speaking publicly out of concern for him. Sure enough, his preparation didn't entirely dispel his nervousness and his "friend" visited him when he started speaking. This time, he was prepared to reassure that "friend" that he was ready to take on the challenge. As he started speaking, he felt his fears dissipating, and he was able to speak with confidence.

Through reframing and other exercises within the course, Michael developed a positive attitude towards public speaking. While the stammer did not disappear, Michael said, "I see stammering now as a signal to slow down. It even can break the monotony of my delivery."

It's been three years since Michael has completed the course, but he still keeps in touch with me. He has completed a Ph.D. and now works as a lecturer.

Eating Vegetables

One of my online students, Andrea, openly admitted to having a short temper. However, since embarking on this course, she shared that she developed a new perspective. She now actively seeks hidden opportunities in situations that might otherwise provoke her anger, often finding herself smiling at the positive thoughts that emerge.

Occasionally, when anger still rears its head, she approaches it differently, as illustrated by this example involving her daughter. "My daughter seems to be on a mission to test me, provoke me and try my patience," Andrea said. Despite attempting to remain patient, her daughter always found ways to push her buttons. Discussing her plight with another course participant, Andrea had a revelation. She decided to edit her internal story from "My daughter is on a mission to annoy me" to "My daughter is simply expressing her emotions." So, the next day, despite coming home tired with a slight headache and the temptation just to zone out, Andrea took a deep breath and consciously decided to keep a positive attitude while dealing with her daughter. "I was determined to meet her on her own terms," she said. Although the daughter started with her usual refusal to listen to her mother's instructions, Andrea managed to stay calm. "I stayed in tune with my emotions, and whenever I felt anger creeping in, I took a deep breath, one of many, and maintained my patience. No tears, no anger—just plenty of smiles and love. This completely turned the situation around. I even convinced her to eat cauliflower, which is a huge achievement because anything from the "green" side is usually her enemy. The following day, I repeated the process. I explained to her that I didn't want to get upset or angry but rather wanted us to be great friends. I asked for her help and requested that she follow my lead. She smiled at me and said, "Okay, mom." Mission accomplished."

It is remarkable to see such results when we trust the process of reframing and editing our internal narrative and have the discipline to go through it.

Finding Love and Getting Married

Another story that is worth sharing is that of Paul, a young man living in Tanzania. He was among the first students to join the *Success with Emotional Intelligence* course. The course helped him be aware of himself, have more self-management and social awareness skills, and develop relationships with others.

At the outset, Paul grappled with a common human struggle - the fear of rejection in matters of love. For three long years, he harboured unspoken affection for a young lady, hindered by the weight of his apprehensions. After watching the lecture on emotional intelligence, which taught that all emotions are okay, he finally gathered the courage to confess his love for her.

The course instilled a fundamental principle: the recognition that all emotions, including vulnerability and fear, are not only natural but also deserving of understanding and expression. Armed with this newfound insight, Paul found the strength to confront his fear and courageously express his love. He offered a ring as a symbol of his commitment and, to his joy, received an enthusiastic acceptance of his proposal.

In a heartwarming twist, Paul's beloved shared his feelings, openly expressing her love and eagerness to build a life together. When she asked about the wellspring of his newfound courage, Paul attributed his transformation to the profound insights he had gleaned from the *Success with Emotional Intelligence* course.

Paul's journey was so transformative that he felt compelled to share his story on the course's website. In a spirit of generosity, he extended an open invitation to all course participants to join in the celebration of his wedding in Tanzania.

The culmination of this remarkable journey was Paul's wedding celebration in December 2013. This story serves as a vivid reminder that by cultivating emotional intelligence, individuals can not only overcome internal barriers but also enrich their lives and relationships, leading to lasting happiness and fulfilment.

Paul's engagement

Seeing the Light Again

In the remarkable journey of Islam Ali, we encounter another profound transformation. Islam, hailing from Jordan, enrolled in not one but two of my Massive Open Online Courses (MOOCs), *Success with Emotional Intelligence* and *Global Entrepreneurship.* Her story illustrates the power of the principles of emotional intelligence in overcoming adversity and fostering personal growth.

Islam, a graduate in Mechatronic Engineering, faced a challenging reality. The economic climate in her region and the unfamiliarity of the traditional industry with her field of study left her unemployed for seven long years. This prolonged struggle led to a deep sense of depression and pessimism, with even minor setbacks feeling like insurmountable disasters. While she never contemplated suicide, she gained insight into the emotional turmoil that suicidal individuals endure. Each passing birthday was a painful reminder of unfulfilled years, and she yearned for something to be proud of.

However, a profound shift occurred when Islam embarked on her MOOC journey. She found herself immersed in a global community of learners. The immediate happiness and satisfaction she derived from the courses were remarkable. She consumed knowledge with a voracious appetite, watching seven lectures within the first week. Engaging in assignments, group work, and mental exercises, Islam's journey into self-discovery began.

One pivotal aspect of her transformation was understanding and naming her emotions. Though initially challenged by the concept of "Brain Rewiring" due to her mental state, Islam persevered. After just one week of these activities, she began to experience a noticeable change in her perspective. A sense of happiness and hopefulness became constants in her life.

With newfound optimism, Islam made the decision to enrol in the *Global Entrepreneurship* MOOC. Recognising that engineers could benefit from mastering business skills, she realised that her engineering background need not limit her to the engineering industry. Her vision crystallised: She aspired to become an educator with an engineer's mindset, shaping generations of successful and content individuals. During the course, she collaborated with a fellow student from Sudan to launch a programme that fostered connections between students of the same age in Jordan and Sudan.

Embracing her passion for education, Islam now plans to pursue a higher diploma in Curriculum and Teaching Methods. She seeks training at an institution that imparts electrical engineering principles to children through innovative methods. Her long-term aspirations now include establishing her own school with a unique curriculum and teaching approach. She attributes much of this transformative thinking to her participation in the MOOCs I offered.

In Islam's journey, we find a testament to the enduring principles of human development, where resilience, emotional intelligence, and the pursuit of meaningful goals converge to illuminate a path from despair to hope, from stagnation to growth, and from self-doubt to boundless possibilities.

Achieving a Mindset Breakthrough

Shannon, one of my online students, offers a compelling journey of personal transformation. Her narrative reflects the potential of optimism, resilience and the power of positive thinking to shape one's life.

Shannon, introspective and honest, acknowledges that confidence has not been a defining trait in her life. She attributes this struggle to her tumultuous upbringing, marked by emotional trauma and a difficult family environment. Her early years were overshadowed by fear, with a father and brothers who inflicted emotional hardships upon her. Their relentless belittlement, exclusion, and mockery of her interests left her feeling isolated and burdened.

The separation of her parents placed her under her mother's care, but her father's continued instability strained their relationship. Her brothers perpetuated their father's example, subjecting her to relentless emotional torment. This pattern persisted into her early adulthood, with her brothers going so far as to sabotage her academic pursuits.

Shannon's relationship with her father reached a breaking point, leading to years of silence and estrangement. However, when her father was diagnosed with a terminal illness, she endeavoured to mend their stormy bond. Paradoxically, his passing left her grappling with guilt and depression, revealing the complex layers of their relationship.

Shannon found solace in her deepening connection with her mother, but tragedy struck again when her mother passed away in 2013. This loss plunged her into a profound depression, prompting her to return to her hometown.

Employed at a local car dealership, Shannon's emotional struggles persisted, eventually putting her job in jeopardy. She reached a breaking point, attempting self-harm but immediately regretting her decision. The experience led to a crucial turning point in her journey, with medical intervention offering a lifeline to recovery.

A significant emotional breakthrough awaited Shannon in 2016 when she encountered the *Success with Emotional Intelligence* course. This transformative experience empowered her to identify areas requiring development and heightened her self-awareness. Notably, the "Brain Rewiring" exercises became a cornerstone of her transformation, reshaping her mindset from doubt, drama and negativity to confidence, gratitude and positivity.

With newfound emotional resilience, Shannon became committed to removing toxic relationships from her life and challenging her inner critic. She found support and validation in the course community, experiencing a shift in her perspective on life. She felt encouraged to share her dreams, which she had long concealed out of fear of ridicule.

Living without Regrets

Deborah's life journey underscores the profound impact of self-awareness and empathy on personal growth and societal change. Her upbringing in a seemingly ideal family environment, where values and morality were paramount, belied a crucial aspect of emotional neglect. While her parents instilled virtue and spirituality, emotional expression was notably absent. As a result, Deborah grew up internalising her feelings, leading to her introverted nature and difficulties in social interactions.

Even as she transitioned into her own family life, mirroring her parents' values, Deborah remained oblivious to the importance of emotional intelligence. This unawareness came to a head when a distressing incident occurred at her children's school. Her oldest son's involvement in bomb threats shocked her, prompting her to reflect on her own emotional upbringing.

Deborah's revelation that her children, like herself, had learned to bury their emotions struck a chord. The consequences of emotional suppression unfolded as her son's troubles with the law escalated, leaving her dealing with regret and self-blame. Instead of dwelling on her past choices, she embraced emotional awareness and empathy as guiding principles in her life.

As her children grew and started their own families, Deborah embarked on a transformative journey through the *Success with Emotional Intelligence* course. This experience allowed her to recognise the void in her childhood and her parenting, spurring personal growth and self-discovery.

Deborah's newfound emotional intelligence illuminated the path towards gratitude and cherishing the opportunity to share her story. She emphasised the capacity of emotional awareness and divine grace to bring about positive change, emphasising the idea that, indeed, bad things can happen to good people.

The course instilled in Deborah the ability to make choices confidently and decisively, breaking free from the shackles of indecision. Once marked by dependency, her relationship with her husband evolved into a secure partnership where both could make independent decisions. She embraced the concept that not all decisions needed to be perfect; the journey of taking risks became a source of joy.

Today, Deborah has transformed herself into a compassionate life coach, extending her wisdom to help abused women and children make better choices. Her belief that life's challenges offer opportunities for growth resonates deeply with the emotional intelligence principles embodied in our course.

Inspired by her journey, Deborah actively advocates for the integration of emotional intelligence into the education system, recognising its potential to empower individuals to navigate life's complexities.

Giving a Hand for Life

Bashirat's remarkable story, as depicted through the lens of developing emotional intelligence, exemplifies the transformative power of self-awareness, resilience, and empathy.

Living in Abuja, Nigeria, Bashirat's life has been marked by a series of profound battles. Her journey includes the tragic loss of her mother, sister, and aunt in a car accident, leaving her with limited emotional support, and later, the painful loss of her husband and father, further intensifying her emotional challenges.

Before these losses, Bashirat was diligently pursuing her M.Sc. thesis. However, the weight of grief cast a pervasive shadow over her ability to concentrate. Forgetfulness and persistent fatigue became her constant companions. Despite a five-month leave of absence from her academic pursuits, progress remained elusive, and the thought of giving up crossed her mind. Yet, she clung to the memory of her earlier academic achievements, determined not to let her dreams slip away.

It was at this critical juncture that Bashirat embarked on a journey of self-discovery through her enrolment in the *Success with Emotional Intelligence* course. While initially wrestling with the course's modules on "Brain Rewiring" and "My Emotions Toda," her unwavering persistence bore fruit. Her emotional landscape shifted from disappointment to gratitude, and her physical exhaustion transformed into robust health. This transformation marked a deep and authentic change in her perspective on life.

As Bashirat became more self-aware, she began to find comfort in life's simple pleasures. She learned to listen to her body and mind, channelling her energy when she was mentally sharp and recognising the need for rest when fatigue or stress encroached. Her vocational pursuits, both online and offline, gained new purpose and impact. She realised that her life story held inherent power.

One of the most challenging aspects of this transformation was coming to terms with the loss of her husband and father, her pillars of support. Bashirat refused to conform to societal expectations dictating her life as a widow. She questioned the notion that her life should end with their passing. Her strength and unwavering faith during these trying times garnered recognition and admiration from those around her.

Bashirat now understands that her turbulent life experiences serve a higher purpose: to inspire and positively impact others who have faced similar emotional traumas. She has transformed her vulnerabilities into stepping stones toward success and extended her hand to assist others on their journeys.

Through the *Success with Emotional Intelligence* course, Bashirat gained the tools to guide others in finding their own paths of self-discovery. She established a social enterprise focused on empowering, educating and coaching women and young people. Her mission centres on reshaping mindsets and enhancing emotional awareness, empowering individuals to unlock their potential and lead fulfilling lives, particularly women and girls. She has played a pivotal role in helping these women launch small businesses, enabling them to provide for their essential needs.

Bashirat firmly believes that her past traumatic experiences uniquely equip her to make a difference and inspire those who have endured similar hardships, especially those teetering on the brink of giving up on life. She boldly declares, "I am a different person now because I refuse to be defined by vulnerability. I've transformed vulnerability into success and am committed to helping others do the same." After navigating these trials and making a profound impact, she describes her current state with insightful clarity:

Mentally: Active
Emotionally: Inspired
Relationally: Grateful
Spiritually: Connected
Vocationally: Fulfilled
Physically: Healthy

Bashirat with the people in her community

In her conclusion, Bashirat embraces the fresh harmony with her emotions, declaring, "I've connected with my emotions; they complete me."

The stories shared above are just a glimpse of the numerous remarkable examples within our course community. These individuals have embraced the language of change, reshaping their internal narratives to achieve success, effectiveness, and happiness. I am deeply honoured by the trust they have placed in our course community and profoundly grateful for their willingness to share their stories with all of us. It is evident that I take immense pride in these course participants and their generous contributions. If you're interested in exploring our course further, please feel free to visit:

https://www.openlearning.com/courses/Success

12

Working with Artificial Intelligence

"A.I. won't take your job. It's somebody using A.I. that will take your job."
Richard Baldwin

In an interview with the BBC in December 2014, the late Stephen Hawking said: "The development of full artificial intelligence could spell the end of the human race. It would take off on its own and re-design itself at an ever-increasing rate. Humans, who are limited by slow biological evolution, couldn't compete and would be superseded."

While concerns regarding Artificial Intelligence, as with any emerging technology, are not new, the endorsement of these concerns by figures like Stephen Hawking lends them additional gravity. There is a consensus that Artificial Intelligence isn't an ordinary technological advancement. While previous technologies have harboured the capacity for both positive and negative outcomes, the ultimate responsibility in determining their applications has always resided with humans. A knife, for instance, can serve culinary purposes or inflict harm, while atomic energy can either fuel cities or obliterate them. Whether for better or worse, humans have historically maintained control.

What sets Artificial Intelligence apart, making it exceptionally potent, is its capability to learn, function and manage itself independently of human oversight. It's worth remembering that what we've seen with ChatGPT and other generative A.I. is just a glimpse of the potential of this technology. The possibilities that lie ahead within the next decade or two are beyond our current comprehension.

The fundamental question before us is: Can we steer the course of Artificial Intelligence? If the answer is affirmative, what values, skills, and mindsets must we cultivate to retain relevance and authority over our destiny? Are we prepared to instil and apply these attributes to as broad a population as possible?

These inquiries hold profound significance; in fact, they could be of existential import. The culmination of rapid technological advancements alongside unparalleled environmental, economic, and geopolitical complexities are reconfiguring not solely the world of work but the entirety of our world in its various facets.

I personally have a deep faith in humanity and hold the conviction that we can indeed maintain dominion over Artificial Intelligence. Moreover, I firmly believe that harnessing and leveraging this technology will equip us to tackle the paramount challenges of our era. Nevertheless, I am mindful that the outcomes I champion are not predestined, and the concerns expressed by Steven Hawking and others are undeniably grounded.

I maintain that long-term and substantial investments in nurturing human potential are imperative to foster individuals endowed with the necessary intellectual, emotional and ethical capacities to function in today's world. These attributes are essential to envisage and actualise a better world—a sustainable, equitable, and enjoyable one. This book has been a humble attempt to delineate what actions leaders must undertake to avert the dystopian future that some forecast.

Our current situation calls for strong and purpose-driven leadership at all levels so that we can define our responses to the world's challenges. Key among them is how to enhance and elevate our human existence, consciousness, and capabilities to remain in control of our technologies.

This chapter will provide some easy-to-follow guidelines to safely and effectively use the large language models type of generative A.I. for work and school.

A.I. at School and Work

Commentators have been talking for a while about how A.I. will change our lives, and we might be standing on the brink of that imminent transformation. Within 40 days of its launch, ChatGPT managed to attract more than 10 million daily users, surpassing Instagram, which took 355 days to achieve 10 million registered users.

Higher education is the first sector that is feeling the impact of this technology. With ChatGPT reported to pass the bar exam and successfully complete MBA exam papers from Wharton, educators will need to develop more personalised and authentic types of assessment if they want to be able to quality assure learning in this new environment. The business sector will also bear the brunt of change as A.I. continually advances in its capacity to handle activities such as report writing, data analysis, market research, presentations and more. As A.I. capabilities progress, many tasks could potentially become fully automated, inevitably impacting human employment opportunities.

Back to the quotation at the beginning of this chapter. "A.I. won't take your job", said Richard Baldwin, an economist, at the World Economic Forum's Growth Summit in Geneva in May 2023. But his following sentence wasn't so reassuring – "It's somebody using A.I. that will take your job." He's right, of course – at least for the time being.

Now that generative A.I., such as ChatGPT and Google's Bard, can perform many intellectual tasks with considerable speed and competency, it is a little wonder that human jobs are considered at risk. However, A.I. is not infallible – just ask Peter LoDuca. LoDuca, a lawyer, learned this the hard way when he was representing a client suing Avianca Airlines in New York federal court, claiming injuries from being hit by a cart during a 2019 flight. LoDuca decided to use ChatGPT to help him with his legal research and ended up citing eight prior cases, all of which turned out to be fabricated by the software. This ended up not only being embarrassing but highly damaging for the case.

This phenomenon, when generative A.I. produces what appears to be factual and relevant information that is totally confabulated, is called "hallucination." A.I. researchers are still working on eliminating this.

So now, what should we do to guarantee we can use A.I. to extend and enhance our capabilities while ensuring we do not fall prey to its shortcomings? Below is a list of 10 things that we can start with:

Know Yourself

It is essential to recognise that in order for us to add authentic value, we need to know who we are, what our purpose is and how we wish to mobilise this purpose into a positive impact on the world. This has always been a valid ambition, but in the age of A.I., it is becoming an existential necessity not only to differentiate the human output from that of the machine but also to enable us to remain anchored and motivated in an era that is categorised by being Volatile, Uncertain, Complex and Ambiguous (VUCA).

I believe that the ultimate value is human by definition, and this ultimate value will always be in our realm. Our unique capabilities to be self-aware, purpose-driven, empathetic, and emotionally intelligent and our propensity to be fair, connected and motivated will become more critical. These aspects of our lives will need to be intentionally cultivated further through our education systems and business practices.

Humans bring value to life and its endeavours by applying three types of capabilities: physical labour, cognitive labour and emotional labour. Whatever we do will require combinations of these three labours. The history of human civilisation and progress can be seen as a journey of the attempts to get our technology to replace us. We first managed to create tools and machines that were faster, stronger, and more accurate than us, largely displacing us from the physical domain of work. With the latest A.I. development, the transition of the machine into the cognitive domain is reaching a critical stage.

During the prehistoric era, humans spent most of their time either collecting food or defending themselves against predators or other people. With the invention of agriculture, people had time to spare for the first time in history, which led to further innovations, including but not limited to the wheel, writing, cities and art. Harnessing the power of steam during the Industrial Revolution had a similar effect on life, with higher standards of living and more time to spare for leisure and other pursuits such as longer education years, hobbies and culture. With A.I. promising to do more cognitive heavy lifting for us, we are at a fork in the road of our civilisation. We have the option of reinventing our education, economy, community, business and government to encourage a greater pursuit of what really matters to us - the fulfilment of our ultimate potential through discovering and articulating our purpose and working towards mobilising it to a positive impact on the world. In this pivotal era, we must harness A.I.'s power to facilitate self-care, foster collective well-being and safeguard our environment. As Stephen Hawking emphasised, the alternative path bears cautionary implications and prompts us to tread with circumspection.

That is why when dealing and working with A.I., knowing ourselves, our values and what we stand for are foundational and essential first steps.

Sharing Private or Confidential Information with A.I.

Generative A.I. is a very powerful conversational tool. People are already using it to help them with school assignments, work projects and even emotional support. Whatever you use it for, do not share private or confidential information with the generative A.I., as all the material you share with A.I. will become part of its training content. For example, if you are working on developing a new marketing strategy for your employer or client, do not share names of customers or previous sales data that are not already available in the public domain.

Sharing privileged information related to your business or that of your clients or associated with confidential projects can be considered serious misconduct by your employer. You will need to check with your employer or school to know if there are specific guidelines for the use of generative A.I.

Provide Effective Prompts

When you utilise generative A.I. to help you with work projects or educational and school tasks, the natural language inputs you use to interact with the system so that it may generate the output or information you are seeking are called "prompts." The structure, nature and quality of these prompts play a pivotal role in guiding the A.I.'s responses and outputs. Prompts can be questions, requests, instructions, examples or information.

When interacting with A.I., whether in written or conversational forms, ensure that your prompts are characterised by clarity, directness and specificity. By furnishing the context and constraints of your inquiry, along with exemplars of the desired output, you can enhance the likelihood of obtaining valuable results. Comprehensive prompts foster a clearer understanding of your requirements, enabling the generative A.I. to produce responses that are more cohesive and pertinent.

A strategic approach involves presenting your prompts in complete sentences, particularly when tackling intricate topics. Breaking down multifaceted subjects into distinct components within your prompts aids the A.I. in comprehending the nuances of your query. This, in turn, contributes to the generation of answers and responses that are more comprehensive and coherent, aligning with your specific needs.

Fact Check

No matter how convincing the output of the generative A.I. is, make sure that you check the produced facts before sharing them or using them as a basis for analysis or decision-making. Remember, A.I. can hallucinate, and lawyer Peter LoDuca's case should serve as a warning. When I was working on a research project that attempts to quantify the role of having a clear sense of purpose in self-motivation, I asked ChatGPT to provide me with a list of related research papers to use as a starting point for my literature review. It came back with a list of titles and specified the names of the authors and the journals where these papers are supposedly published. The list looked impressive and credible. The academic in me insisted on fact-checking the list, and none of the references cited was real.

A.I. researchers are working on minimising hallucination, but this is a challenging task as the ability to create plausible fabrications is rooted in the same algorithms that enable A.I. to be creative.

Do Not Copy and Paste

When we teach academic writing, we tell our students to paraphrase the text they intend to use, if it came from the internet or from other reference materials. This is still valid and wise advice when dealing with the content created using A.I. Whether you are a student working on an assignment or a professional trying to increase your productivity and effectiveness using A.I., often it is very tempting just to copy and paste what is produced. Resist this temptation. It would be best if you used A.I. to inspire you rather than replace you. A.I. can generate very interesting connections, view matters from angles you did not consider and even improve grammar and check for typos. These can be beneficial enhancements to your work, and they can help you enrich it and improve your productivity. So, make sure to rewrite what you wish to adopt using your own language and consider A.I. as an assistant or a partner you can brainstorm with.

Be Transparent

Sometimes, the work generated by A.I. is made for a low-stake or secondary project, and your assessment is that you can use what is produced without modification. Ensure you mention that clearly to those assessing or using your work. They will usually appreciate your transparency and professionalism. Depending on the nature of the work, you may still need to do fact-checks, though.

Now, whenever I receive legal or public relations texts that I need to approve on behalf of our university, I ask the originator of the work to disclose if they have used A.I. in its production. I believe that as the guidelines and protocols surrounding A.I. usage continue to evolve, such declarations will progressively become a standard aspect of the work process. This proactive declaration approach will promote accountability and build more trust.

Ensure You Provide Value

Bear in mind that regardless of whether you're a student undergoing evaluation, an employee receiving compensation or a participant in the gig economy, those overseeing your work—be it a teacher, supervisor, or client—anticipate that your contributions add genuine value to the tasks at hand. If what you are submitting is merely the outcome of A.I. solutions, the end users might consider implementing these solutions themselves to carry out the required tasks. It's crucial to ensure that the distinct value you bring is discernible.

Achieving this can involve tapping into your unique personal experiences and perspectives or referencing and integrating current events that A.I. might not be equipped to grasp. It's vital to recognise that the ultimate value generated, exchanged and assessed is inherently a product of human interaction. This aspect remains our enduring strength and advantage.

Use Polite Language

It was explored earlier in this book how the vocabulary and the language we regularly use drive our internal narrative and often end up shaping who we are and how we perceive the world and interact with others. This central role of language is true for A.I. as well. Mo Gawdat, the author of *Scary Smart* [1], outlined in his book how A.I. is learning from us with every interaction. He proposed that the only way for us to instil positive values into the A.I. algorithms is to behave positively ourselves. Therefore, when conversing with A.I. it is essential for us to use polite language. The language we adopt when using A.I. will be utilised to train the system, and we want the system to be trained positively. It is also generally nice to keep the conversation professional.

It is now well-established that algorithms are capable of picking up even our subconscious biases. A.I. systems used for screening job applications as part of hiring purposes, for example, started to screen out people from certain ethnic backgrounds simply because the "training materials" provided to them (basically a large number of human decisions made on previous job applications) had that hidden bias against these ethnic groups. So, as our machines see through us and learn from us, we need to bring the best versions of ourselves to the table, including the most professional and positive versions of our language.

Stay Out of Harm's Way

Avoid using the A.I. to create inappropriate, harmful or offensive content, even if you are just experimenting. While generative A.I. systems are now trained to refuse requests to create harmful or offensive content, such as hate speech, it is advisable to refrain from engaging in these types of interactions. We must remember that our actions have legal and moral implications when dealing with our most potent technological advancement.

Celebrate the "Made by Humans" Brand

Finally, if the work you're producing has been crafted without any contribution from Artificial Intelligence, it's beneficial to provide an explicit declaration affirming its human origin. A statement such as "This work was exclusively created by humans without any involvement of artificial intelligence" can illuminate the process for your audience, demonstrating your commitment to transparency. As we mentioned multiple times in this book, we are the ultimate judges of value, and we seem to put a premium on things made using our clever craftsmanship. We have the best cameras, but we still value paintings made by artists, and we are willing to pay more for handmade products and artefacts. The key is what we are creating needs to be useful, clever, unique and original.

Adopting this view, we can see that A.I. and automation are pushing us in the direction of realising our highest potential and urging us to hold ourselves to higher standards. This can be stressful, of course, and requires us to make uncomfortable changes, but it represents a more positive mindset towards dealing with the A.I. revolution.

It's worth noting that this chapter serves as an initial attempt to offer practical insights into effectively collaborating with Artificial Intelligence. Undoubtedly, the protocols for the effective and safe usage of A.I. will continue to evolve, advance and adapt as the technology progresses and our capability to use it is enhanced and improved.

(This page is intentionally left blank)

Epilogue:
What Story Will You Tell?

"Those who tell the stories rule the world."

Hopi American Indian proverb

Thanks a lot for completing this book. I really do hope that you have enjoyed it and that you feel more optimistic and empowered. We went on a short yet rich journey together where we explored how we think, feel, perceive our world and behave, and the role of the stories we tell and the language we use in all of that. We also examined the biological, psychological and social roots of why stories are so crucial to our existence. I hope that by now, you will appreciate the importance of our stories in shaping our identities, both individually and collectively.

We explored the different levels of human existence, performance and development, namely, language, narratives, awareness and regulation and provided techniques to influence them positively. We moved on to telling the stories of people who have managed to change their lives positively by adopting the philosophy and techniques outlined in this book.

Our tour was concluded by examining ways to leverage Artificial Intelligence, outlining some tips to help support its effective use for work and learning.

The story of human civilisation is that of an epic journey driven by our yearning to discover our purpose and mobilise it into a positive impact on the world. We had our dark moments, of course, but the overall trajectory is positive. We achieved mind-blowing cultural and technological advancements, and, in the process, we were able to make machines that surpassed us in physical strength, precision and speed, rendering these machines superior to us in the physical domain. We are doing the same in the cognitive domain with computers, algorithms and A.I. surpassing, or moving towards surpassing, our capabilities in the fields of information processing and decision-making, among others. This is leaving us no choice but to question who we really are. Are we our bodies, our intellect and intelligence, or do we transcend all of that?

Artificial Intelligence is but the latest and one of the biggest disruptors humanity has to deal with. It has the capacity to help us truly unleash our full potential and address the biggest challenges of our time. It also can be used to inflict harm at scales that we have not witnessed before. Now more than ever, we must enhance the human capacity for love, wisdom and compassion. We need to tell the most empowering stories about ourselves and the world we live in.

I hope this book will be helpful to you as you direct your own story and help others direct theirs. As you do that, I would love to hear from you and know about what stories you are telling. You can reach me at mushtak.alatabi@gmail.com

Dream Big. Be Different. Have Fun

Notes

Chapter 1: Homo Relator: What Makes Us Human

1. National Academy of Engineering, 2008. *NAE Grand Challenges for Engineering.* [Online] National Academy of Engineering. Available at: *http://www.engineeringchallenges.org*

2. Taylor, J. B., 2008. *My Stroke of Insight.* [Online] TED: Ideas Worth Spreading. Available at:

   https://www.ted.com/talks/jill_bolte_taylor_s_powerful_stroke_of_insight

3. Gazzaniga, M. S., 2016. *Tales from Both Sides of the Brain: A Life in Neuroscience.* Reprint ed. New York: Ecco.

4. Taylor, J. B., 2009. *My Stroke of Insight: A Brain Scientist's Personal Journey.* New York: Penguin Books.

5. Botkin, J.W., Elmandjra, M., and Malitza, M., 1979. *No Limits to Learning: Bridging the Human Gap.* A Report to the Club of Rome. Pergamon Press.

Chapter 2: What Story Are You Telling

1. Smith, D. L., 2011. *Less than Human: Why We Demean, Enslave and Exterminate Others.* New York: St Martin's Press.

2. Covey, Stephen R., 2020. *The 7 Habits of Highly Effective People.* Simon and Schuster.

Chapter 3: How to Programme a Mind

1. Dweck, C. S., 2007. *Mindset: The New Psychology of Success.* New York: Ballantine Books.

2. Gladwell, M., 2008. *Outliers: The Story of Success.* New York: Little, Brown and Company

3. Sinek, S., 2011. *Start with Why: How Great Leaders Inspire Everyone to Take Action.* New York: Penguin Books.

Chapter 4: Success and Emotional Intelligence

1. Harari, Y. N., 2015. *Sapiens: A Brief History of Humankind.* New York: HarperCollins.

2. Goleman, D., 1995. *Emotional Intelligence.* New York: Bantam Books

3. Goleman, D., 2000. *Working with Emotional Intelligence.* New York: Bantam Books.

4. Pinker, S., 2009. *How the Mind Works.* Reissue ed. New York: W.W. Norton and Company.

5. Wagner, T., 2008. *The Global Achievement Gap: Why Even Our Best Schools Don't Teach the New Survival Skills Our Children Need-and What We Can Do About It.* New York: Basic Books.

6. Helliwell, J., Layard, R., Sachs, J., De Neve, J., Ankin, L., and Wang, S., 2023. *World Happiness Report 2023.*

7. King, V., 2016. *10 Keys to a Happier Living.* Headline Publishing Group.

Chapter 5: Self-Awareness

1. Flaum, J.P., 2010. *When it Comes to Leadership, Nice Guys Finish First – what predicts executive success.* [Online] Green Peak Partners. Available at: *http://greenpeakpartners.com/what-we-think/what-predicts-executive-success-green-peak-and-cornell-university-study*

2. Briñol, P., Petty, R.E., and Wagner, B. 2009. *Body Posture Effects on Self-Evaluation: A Self-Validation Approach.* European Journal of Social Psychology. Volume 39, Issue 6, Pages 1053-1064.

Chapter 7: Self-Management

1. Mischel, W., 2015. *The Marshmallow Test: Why Self-Control is the Engine of Success.* Paperback ed. New York: Little, Brown and Company.

2. Frankl, V. E., 2006. *Man's Search for Meaning.* Boston: Beacon Press.

3. Baumeister, R. F. & Tierney, J., 2012. *Willpower: Rediscover the Greatest Human Strength.* New York: Penguin Books.

4. Ben-Shahar, T., 2007. *Happier: Learn the Secrets to Daily Joy and Lasting Fulfilment.* McGraw-Hill: New York.

5. Estrella, M., 2014. *How a Password Changed My Life.* [Online] The Huffington Post. Available at:

   http://www.huffingtonpost.com/mauricio-estrella/how-a-password-changed-my-life_b_5567161.html

6. Pink, D. H., 2011. *Drive: The Surprising Truth About What Motivates Us.* New York: Riverhead Books.

7. Louis Armstrong, *When You Smile (The Whole World Smiles with You).*

8. Ekman, P., Rosenberg, E.L., 2005. *What the Face Reveals: Basic and Applied Studies of Spontaneous Expression Using the Facial Action Coding System.* 2nd Ed. Oxford University Press: New York.

9. Lewis, M. and Bowler, P. (2009). Botulinum toxin cosmetic therapy correlates with a more positive mood. Journal of Cosmetic Dermatology, 8(1), pp.24-26.

Chapter 8: Relationship Management

1. Waldinger, R., 2015. *What Makes a Good Life? Lessons from the Longest Study on Happiness.* [Online] TED: Ideas Worth Spreading. Available at:

   https://www.ted.com/talks/robert_waldinger_what_makes_a_good_life_l essons_from_the_longest_study_on_happiness

2. Seligman, M. E., 2012. *Flourish: A Visionary New Understanding of Happiness and Well-being.* New York: Free Press.

3. Kohlrieser, G., 2006. *Hostage at the Table.* San Francisco: Jossey-Bass.

4. Brown, J. L., Roderick , T., Lantieri, L. & Aber, J. L., 2004. The Resolving Conflict Creatively Program: A School-Based Social and Emotional Learning Program. In: J. E. Zins, R. P. Weissberg, M. C. Wang & H. J. Walberg, eds. *Building Academic Success on Social and Emotional Learning: What Does the Research Say?.* New York: Teachers College Press, pp. 151-169.

5. Warner, J., 2002. *Aspirations of Greatness: Mapping the Mid-Life Leaders Reconnection to Self and Soul.* New York: Wiley.

6. Granovetter, M.S., 1973. *The Strength of Weak Ties.* American Journal of Sociology. Vol. 78, No. 6, pp. 1360-1380.

Chapter 9: Telling the Story

1. https://significantobjects.com

2. Anderson, C., 2016. *TED Talks: The Official Guide to Public Speaking.* London: Headline Publishing.

3. Gladwell, M., 2000. *The Tipping Point: How Little Things Can Make a Big Difference.* New York: Little, Brown and Company.

4. Heath, C. & Heath, D., 2007. *Made to Stick: Why Some Ideas Take Hold and Others Come Unstuck.* New York: Random House.

5. Gates, B., 2009. *Mosquitoes, Malaria and Education*. [Online] TED: Ideas Worth Spreading. Available at:

    https://www.ted.com/talks/bill_gates_unplugged

6. Weintraub, P., 2010. *The Dr. Who Drank Infectious Broth, Gave Himself an Ulcer, and Solved a Medical Mystery*. [Online] Discover. Available at: *http://discovermagazine.com/2010/mar/07-dr-drank-broth-gave-ulcer-solved-medical-mystery*

Chapter 10: Shoot the Boss: Leadership and Emotional Intelligence

1. Hsieh, T., 2013. *Delivering Happiness: A Path to Profits, Passions, and Purpose*. New York: Grand Central Publishing.

2. Logan, D., King, J. P. & Fischer-Wright, H., 2008. *Tribal Leadership: Leveraging Natural Groupd to Build a Thriving Community*. New York: Collins.

Chapter 12: Working with Artificial Intelligence

1. Gawdat, M., 2021. *Scary Smart: The Future of Artificial Intelligence and How You Can Save Our World*. London: Bluebird Books.

Image Sources

Chapter 1: Homo Relator: What Makes Us Human

A Neuron. Source: Wiki Commons, 2008. Available at: *https://commons.wikimedia.org/wiki/Neuron#/media/File:Derived_Neuron_ schema_with_no_labels.svg*

Chapter 4: Success and Emotional Intelligence

Emotional Intelligence Framework. Source: Goleman, D., 1995. *Emotional Intelligence.* New York: Bantam Books.

Chapter 9: Telling the Story

Picasso's "The Bull". Source: Bennett, J. Available at: *http://www.takeovertime.co*

Index

complex, 3, 8, 12, 13, 32, 73, 104, 111, 116, 126, 129, 137, 167

component, 9, 98, 150

composite, 72, 74

comprehend, 68, 137, 141

computer, 9, 44, 68, 91, 103

conceive, 31, 47

concentrate, 169

concept, 1, 2, 18, 25, 45, 51, 66, 67, 75, 106, 137, 139, 144, 157, 165, 169

conceptual, 4

concrete, 141, 143

confess, 163

confident, 86, 112

conflict, 30, 33, 116, 122, 124, 126-127

confrontation, 98, 102

congruent, 22, 109

conscious, 13, 57, 61

consistent, 85, 101, 135

constitution, 37

context, 17, 34, 38, 65, 84, 135, 157, 178

continue, 31, 35, 44, 48, 56, 58, 60, 68, 78, 143, 180, 183

continuous, 16

control, 2, 12-13, 19, 23, 30, 35, 46-47, 57, 65, 67, 91, 97-100, 102, 111, 173, 175

convergence, 5

convince, 120, 151

cooperation, 134

cooperative, 93

corporate, 72

cortisol, 87, 134

cosmetic, 112, 189

courage, 163-164

course, 1, 2, 6, 54-55, 67, 79-80, 91, 102-103, 108, 117, 143, 157, 159, 161-164, 166-170, 172, 174-175, 183, 186

craft, 25, 57, 61, 133

create, 10, 49, 56, 58, 72, 74, 79, 93, 129, 134-135, 159, 177, 179, 182

creation, 32, 68, 75, 102, 123

creative, 53, 56, 179

creativity, 5, 18, 56, 68

credible, 140, 143, 179

credit, 37, 99, 119, 150, 153

crimes, 30

criminal, 139

crisis, 119, 147, 148

criterion, 77

critic, 84, 167

critical, 1, 27, 45, 52, 101, 108, 123, 129, 137, 170, 177

crossword, 53

cruciverbalist, 53

crystallisation, 157

crystallography, 157

Cuddy, Amy, 87

cultivate, 6, 32, 53, 56, 58, 59, 69-70, 90, 100, 102, 112, 116, 129, 174

culture, 37, 48, 156-157, 177

cure, 141

curiosity, 129

curious, 80, 124

curriculum, 2-3, 6, 47, 148, 166

customer, 61, 90, 152, 153, 155

cystic, 110

D

Dalai Lama, 4, 5

Damon, William, 106

Deborah, 49, 168, 169

deceptive, 22

decide, 1, 65

decision, 13-14, 16, 142, 150, 165, 167, 179, 186

definition, 59, 70, 119, 176

dehumanise, 38

demonstrate, 140

demotivate, 109

denial, 53

denounce, 101

depletion, 100

depression, 23, 165, 167

design, 6, 33, 90, 94, 153, 173

desirable, 61

destinations, 35, 142

destiny, 52, 174

G

GABA, 24
Gallacher, Mike, 52
gallbladder, 110
gallstones, 110
Gates, Bill, 57, 139, 191
Gawdat, Mo, 181, 191
Gazzaniga, Michael, 20, 21, 187
GDP, 72-74
Genentech, 157
genes, 56
genocide, 30
Germany, 149
GIHI, 72, 73
Gladwell, Malcolm, 57, 136, 187, 190
Glenn, Joshua, 133
glutamate, 24
GNH, 72
GNHI, 73
goal, 23, 61, 75, 108-110, 115, 117
God, 31
Goleman, Daniel, 1-2, 38-39, 65, 67,
    71, 78, 90, 100, 188, 192
governance, 73
government, 37, 73-74, 101, 120, 177
GPS, 142
gratification, 97
gratitude, 102, 117, 119, 167-168, 170
Greece, 37

H

habits, 10-12, 32-33, 39, 44, 47, 52, 57-
    58, 72, 77, 104
habitually, 133
hallucination, 176, 179
happiness, 2-4, 8, 23, 26-27, 32, 38, 53-
    54, 59, 70, 72-75, 106, 116, 152, 154,
    164-165, 172, 190
happy, 1, 3, 10, 15-16, 66, 74, 80, 98,
    111, 115, 116, 152-155
Harari, Yuval, 65, 188
Harb, Asma, 51
hardwired, 13, 89, 101
hardwiring, 57

Harvard, 18, 115, 129
Hawking, Stephen, 173-174, 177
health, 4, 23-24, 32, 61, 70-71, 80, 83,
    98, 106, 115, 120, 148, 170
healthcare, 51
healthy, 23-24, 66, 70, 74, 80, 87, 115-
    116, 142
Heath, Chip, 136
Heath, Dan, 136
Heider, Fritz, 89
Himalayas, 72
holistic, 6, 66, 69-70, 73-74
Hollywood, 120, 143
hormone, 24, 87
Hsieh, Tony, 152-153
Huffington Post, 103, 189
human capital, 70, 130

I

IBM, 68
ICT, 103
idea, 22, 78, 103, 120, 136-137, 141-144,
    154, 157, 168
identify, 19, 61, 99, 111, 118, 167
identity, 25, 37, 158
ikigai, 106-107
imagination, 14, 18, 29, 70
imagine, 11, 13, 15, 30, 54, 84, 105,
    126, 134, 136
impact statement, 107, 108
influence, 4, 8, 14, 23, 38, 48, 87, 92,
    98, 116, 119, 134, 185
Ingham, Harrington, 82
innovate, 156
inspiration, 85
inspire, 59, 134, 170-171, 180
instincts, 13, 69
intellect, 80, 186
intelligent, 7, 25, 68, 72, 75, 78, 117,
    119, 147, 176
IQ, 5, 68, 70
Italian, 90